TRANSITION SERVICES FOR STUDENTS
WITH SIGNIFICANT DISABILITIES
IN COLLEGE AND COMMUNITY SETTINGS

PRO-ED Series on Transition

Edited by
J. Patton
G. Blalock
C. Dowdy
T. E. C. Smith

TRANSITION SERVICES FOR STUDENTS WITH SIGNIFICANT DISABILITIES IN COLLEGE AND COMMUNITY SETTINGS

Strategies for Planning, Implementation, and Evaluation

Meg Grigal
Debra A. Neubert
M. Sherril Moon

8700 Shoal Creek Boulevard
Austin, Texas 78757-6897
800/897-3202   Fax 800/397-7633
www.proedinc.com

© 2005 by PRO-ED, Inc.
8700 Shoal Creek Boulevard
Austin, Texas 78757-6897
800/897-3202   Fax 800/397-7633
www.proedinc.com

Library of Congress Cataloging-in-Publication Data

Grigal, Meg.
    Transition services for students with significant disabilities in college and community
    settings : strategies for planning, implementation, and evaluation / Meg Grigal, Debra A.
    Neubert, M. Sherril Moon.
        p. cm. — (PRO-ED series on transition)
    Includes bibliographical references.
    ISBN-13: 978-089079993-2 (alk. paper)
    ISBN-10: 0-89079-993-8 (alk. paper)
    1. Young adults with disabilities—Education (Higher)—United States.   2. Young adults
with disabilities—Vocational guidance—United States.   3. Young adults with disabilities—
Services for—United States.   4. School-to-work transition—United States.   5. Education,
Cooperative—United States.   I. Neubert, Debra A.   II. Moon, M. Sherril, 1952–   III. Title.
IV. Series.
LC4813.G75 2004
371.9′0474—dc22

This book is designed in New Century Schoolbook, Melior, and Helvetica.

Printed in the United States of America

2 3 4 5 6 7 8 9 10 ·   08 07

Contents

List of Reproducible Forms

Preface to the Series

The transition of students from school to adult roles has emerged as one of the most important topics in the fields of special education and rehabilitation. The critical nature of planning for the transition needs of students has also been recognized in the school-to-work, often referred to as the school-to-careers, initiative.

The PRO-ED Series on Transition evolved from a symposium convened in September 1994. Along with the opportunity for professionals interested in the practical aspects of the transition process to discuss many different issues, the symposium produced a series of papers that were originally published in the *Journal of Learning Disabilities* and, subsequently, in a book titled *Transition and Students with Learning Disabilities*. The current series provides transition personnel with practical resources on a variety of topics that are critical to the process of preparing individuals for adulthood. Each book in the series contains valuable, practical information on a specific transition topic. The following is the complete list of titles in the series:

- *Adult Agencies: Linkages for Adolescents in Transition*
- *Assessment for Transitions Planning*
- *Developing Transition Plans*
- *Facilitating the Transition of Students Who Are Deaf or Hard of Hearing*
- *Family Involvement in Transition Planning and Implementation*
- *Follow-Up Studies: A Practitioner's Handbook*
- *Infusing Real-Life Topics into Existing Curricula: Recommended Procedures and Instructional Examples for the Elementary, Middle, and High School Levels*
- *Self-Determination Strategies*
- *Student-Focused Conferencing and Planning*
- *Teaching Occupational Social Skills*
- *Transition from School to Young Adulthood: Basic Concepts and Recommended Practices*
- *Transition Issues Related to Students with Visual Disabilities*
- *Transition to Employment*
- *Transition to Postsecondary Education: Strategies for Students with Disabilities*
- *Transition Services for Students with Significant Disabilities in College and Community Settings*
- *Using Community Transition Teams To Improve Transition Services*
- *Working with Students with Disabilities in Vocational–Technical Settings*

We hope these resources will add to the growing body of material designed to assist professionals involved in the transition process. The books in this series address the need for practical resources on transition that focus solely on specific topics.

—*Jim Patton, Ginger Blalock, Carol Dowdy, and Tom Smith*

Preface

Many, if not most, students exiting the public school system want to go to college. Their experience may consist of taking a few classes at a local community college or attending a 4-year college or university full time. College is seldom an option, however, for students with significant disabilities, such as mental retardation, autism, or multiple disabilities. Traditionally, students with significant disabilities have received transition services in a public high school setting until they are 21 or 22 years old. Although this is an appropriate educational setting for students ages 14 years to 18 years, it may not be the best or most motivating setting for older students with significant disabilities. Parents, researchers, and school system personnel have questioned whether serving students ages 18 to 21 with significant disabilities in high schools leads to a successful transition to adulthood. Instead, they have advocated for providing transition services in the same college and community settings in which these students' peers without disabilities are learning.

The local school system (LSS) is responding to these concerns by providing such opportunities in various college and community settings. Although the LSS often assumes major responsibility for developing and implementing services, other organizations—such as agencies serving adults with disabilities, colleges, and community employers—may also provide resources and support. These transition services have been described in the literature as *programs* in college and community settings (Grigal, Neubert, & Moon, 2001; Hall, Kleinert, & Kearns, 2000; Neubert, Moon, & Grigal, 2002) and as *individual supports* (Hart, Zafft, & Zimbrich, 2001; Page & Chadsey-Rusch, 1995; Tashie, Malloy, & Lichtenstein, 1998).

Regardless of the approach, providing transition services in settings other than the high school supports age-appropriate and inclusive experiences, collaboration and planning among diverse partners, and reallocation of resources and staff. Transition services in these environments offer benefits to students with significant disabilities by (a) increasing their access to new environments and activities and (b) providing opportunities for flexible scheduling and interagency collaboration. The desired outcome is that students with disabilities exit the school system with skills that will allow them to pursue employment opportunities; experience lifelong learning opportunities; and participate in community activities that match their goals, dreams, and interests.

For the past 5 years, we have worked with the staff of local school systems in the United States who were interested in, or actively engaged in, providing transition services to students with significant disabilities through a program approach in a college or community setting. Our work has been supported by Grants H324R990032 and H324R020063 from the U.S. Department of Education, Office of Special Education and Rehabilitative Services (OSERS), and Office of Special Education Programs. These grants funded On-Campus Outreach (OCO), a project designed to investigate and support best transition practices for students ages 18 to 21 with significant disabilities in postsecondary settings.

Through our work on this project, we discovered that few guidelines existed for developing transition services or programs in college and community settings. In addition, personnel actually offering such services or programs had few guidelines for evaluating or expanding their efforts. The OCO staff investigated how programs offering transition services in these settings were set up, what issues arose regarding the daily implementation of services, what barriers occurred to expanding services in response to increased demand, and whether evaluation efforts found outcomes and benefits for these students.

We have compiled our findings into this user-friendly book, which we hope will be used as a resource by school personnel, families, and individuals interested in expanding transition services for students with significant disabilities to college and community settings. The contents of this book have been used in pilot programs in Maryland, Connecticut, and Virginia. In addition, the text and accompanying forms have been reviewed by teachers, transition specialists, and directors of special education programs, who provided us with feedback regarding their format, clarity, and organization.

Our purpose in this book is to provide a framework and strategies for persons who are interested in designing, implementing, or evaluating transition services in a college or community setting for students with significant disabilities. The process of creating these services requires a great deal of collaboration, flexibility, and patience. Most of all, anyone involved in creating new transition services must firmly believe that all services should be based upon each individual student's needs, preferences, and interests. Our premise is that the first step in creating new services is to identify the needs and desires of students. Once these are identified, the focus should shift to identifying the services, supports, and learning environments required to address those needs. Finally, all transition services, regardless of where they are provided, must be monitored and evaluated on a regular basis to ensure successful student outcomes. To reflect these beliefs, this book is organized into three chapters—Chapter 1: Planning and Development, Chapter 2: Implementation, and Chapter 3: Evaluation.

In Chapter 1, we provide a comprehensive overview of the steps for identifying the need for and creating new transition services. These steps include how to create and convene a planning committee; how to conduct needs assessments for current student services and community partnerships; and, if deemed necessary, how to plan for new services or programs outside of the high school.

In Chapter 2, we describe in detail the process of implementing new transition services, focusing on both the policy and procedural aspects of service delivery in a college or community setting, as well as the daily operations entailed in providing such services. This chapter contains a thorough overview of issues, such as staffing, referral, transportation, and budget, that often prove to be stumbling blocks during the planning of new services or programs. In this chapter, we also emphasize matching the college or community setting to students' learning needs so that students have opportunities to learn, work, and engage in leisure activities with individuals without disabilities. Finally, the chapter includes examples of how to manage the complex tasks of scheduling student supports and monitoring student and staff activities.

In Chapter 3, we offer an overview of various methods that may be used to evaluate transition services in college and community settings, such as compiling data on student and staff activities, gauging participant satisfaction, collecting exit data, and conducting follow-up activities. In addition, we address the evaluation process and provide a structure to help school system personnel in determining a schedule for evaluation activities, assigning individuals to collect and compile the information and data, and reviewing and sharing evaluation data with pertinent parties.

Each chapter contains blank forms that may be copied and used by readers. These forms are numbered sequentially and will be referred to in the narrative with a title and page number; for example, Form 1: Planning Committee Contact Sheet (see p. 24). In addition, each form is available on the accompanying compact disc in Microsoft Excel format. Users thus will be able to modify each form to meet their individual needs; fill out and update forms via the computer; attach and e-mail forms to others; and maintain computer records of their planning, implementation, and evaluation efforts.

In some cases, examples of completed forms will be provided as figures in the text. We have also included a number of profiles that illustrate how the strategies suggested in this book could be implemented by a public school system. For the sake of simplicity, we used a fictional school system—Buckman County Public Schools—to demonstrate the use of our forms and recommendations. Each example is based, however, upon real experiences we have had with school system personnel involved in this process. Finally, we have compiled a bibliography that we believe will be helpful to individuals interested in learning more about this form of transition service delivery.

Acknowledgments

First and foremost we wish to thank the teachers and staff members of 19 programs throughout the state of Maryland for sharing their experiences with us and with each other. It is through their collective vision that students with significant disabilities have been given the chance to broaden their horizons into the postsecondary world. We appreciate their dedication, creativity, and continued commitment to helping their students achieve desired outcomes.

We also want to thank Dennis Snyder for initiating the practice of gathering teachers from across the state to network and discuss the issues they face in supporting students in college and community settings. This work was the foundation of our project's biannual Networking Teacher Forums, which continue to provide teachers with an arena for sharing ideas, solving problems, and discussing issues associated with providing transition services in a college or community setting.

We offer a special thanks to our project officer from the Office of Special Education Programs, Debra Price-Ellingstad, whose constant support and positive feedback affirmed our belief in the importance of this project.

We would also like to thank our colleagues from around the country who are working on increasing access to postsecondary education for students with significant disabilities. Your work is vital and helps broaden expectations for these students and the people who work with them. We extend our gratitude to Debra Hart of the Institute for Community Inclusion, University of Massachusetts, Boston, and Children's Hospital Boston; Cate Weir of the Institute on Disability, University of New Hampshire; and Teresa Whelley and Bob Stodden of the National Center for the Study of Postsecondary Educational Supports, University of Hawaii.

Finally, we thank the reviewers who provided us with feedback regarding the readability and utility of this book: Deborah Ward and Mike Jones of Howard County Public Schools in Maryland, Terri Crawford of Allegany County Public Schools in Maryland, Ginny Brennan and Ann Marie Cook of Fairfax County Public Schools in Virginia, Kay Mosser of Monroe Public Schools in Connecticut, and Joyce Emmett of Danbury Public Schools in Connecticut.

CHAPTER 1
Planning and Development

Traditionally, students with significant disabilities receive transition services in a public high school setting until they are 21 or 22 years old. Although this is an appropriate setting for students ages 14 to 18 years, it may not be the most appropriate or motivating place for students with significant disabilities who are 19 to 21 years of age (hereafter referred to as "older students"). Because there are questions regarding whether serving older students with significant disabilities in high schools leads to successful transition experiences, more people are advocating that transition services be provided in college and community settings instead.

Local school systems are responding to these concerns by providing opportunities for older students with significant disabilities to receive transition services in a variety of college and community settings. Providing such services in these settings supports age-appropriate and inclusive experiences, collaboration and planning among diverse partners, and reallocation of resources and staff. The goal is for these students to leave the school system with the skills they need to pursue employment, educational opportunities, and community activities that match their goals, dreams, and interests.

Creating new transition services in college and community settings for older students with significant disabilities takes a great deal of time, planning, and collaboration among various members of the school system and the community. More than anything, the planning process will require leadership and patience. Whoever spearheads this endeavor will need to be committed to a long-term process, one that may require repeated explanations to individuals who do not understand or support the need for change.

Administrators, parents, or college personnel may pose questions such as, "Why should students with significant disabilities go to college?" or "What are they going to get out of this?" Changing expectations and expanding horizons for students who receive special education services has always been a struggle. Personnel in many school systems continue to struggle with providing access to general education classrooms and curricula, and creating access to college and community environments will be a similar challenge. It will require changes not only in location but also in funding, staffing, transportation, and community partnerships. The individuals involved in such planning must remember, however, that the purpose is not simply to create access to new learning environments. A major goal should be to create opportunities for students to meet their individual desires, become integrated and involved in their post–high school community, and achieve an adult lifestyle that makes them happy.

1. Local school system (LSS) director of special education and other special education administrators/coordinators

2. LSS teachers and department chairs of high schools sending students

3. LSS principal(s)

4. Personnel from other school systems who may want to collaborate in creating new services

5. Community-based instructors/work coordinators/transition specialists

6. Related-services personnel, such as therapists, counselors, and paraprofessionals

7. Parents

8. Local agencies serving adults (e.g., community not-for-profit organizations, vocational or residential support providers, The Arc)

9. Personnel from local community colleges or universities

10. Teachers or staff members of existing programs in postsecondary settings

11. Vocational rehabilitation or developmental disabilities case management representatives

12. Advocacy organization representatives

13. Recent graduate or student with a significant disability

14. Others (list):

Figure 1.1. Potential candidates for membership on a planning committee.

PLANNING COMMITTEE

The first step in planning or developing transition services in a college or community setting is to create and convene a planning committee. Members of this committee should include people from any of the environments where students may receive support or services, including advocacy groups, the local schools, the college or community site, students' homes, adult community service agencies, and state case management agencies (e.g., for vocational rehabilitation or developmental disabilities). Once the committee members have been identified, a contact list and a meeting schedule can be created.

Identify Planning Committee Members

We suggest that school system personnel, students, and parents who are spearheading this process meet initially to determine which individuals should be included on the planning committee. In choosing these people, variables to consider are familiarity with the students, availability for attending meetings, the potential for providing services or supports, and an ability to make a long-term commitment. Once planning begins, the initial committee list may change, with some members leaving and new persons joining. A list of individuals to consider is provided in Figure 1.1.

Create a Contact List

Once the committee has been organized, we suggest creating a contact list to facilitate ongoing communication among its members. Form 1: Planning Committee Contact Sheet (see p. 24) may be used to create a master list of all members, with their names, positions, organizations, telephone and fax numbers, and e-mail addresses. Each member of the committee should have a copy of this list, which can be maintained and updated by a designated person. An example of a completed contact list is provided in Figure 1.2.

Create a Meeting Schedule for the Committee

An initial meeting of the entire committee should be scheduled to discuss goals and create an agenda for future meetings. Creating a meeting schedule will also help members to see the amount of their time they may have to commit. One committee member should be identified as the main contact when scheduling conflicts arise and individual members are not able to attend meetings. As planning progresses, the entire committee may not always need to convene. Instead, smaller groups (e.g., subcommittees) of individuals involved in similar aspects of the planning can set their own meetings.

Communicate Committee Goals

Obviously, committee members should clearly understand the mission and purpose of the committee. Initially, the mission may simply be to review current transition services or to discuss potential models for program expansion. Whatever the mission, it should be clearly identified from the outset. As noted previously, members must also know the amount of time that it will take to achieve this purpose. For example, if the mission is to oversee the creation of a new program, members may expect to meet for a year or more. The mission statement should be reviewed at the first meeting and whenever new members attend their first meeting. As the goals of the committee change from planning and development to monitoring and evaluation, the mission statement should be updated to reflect those changes. At that point, the committee will change from a planning group to an advisory group. A sample mission statement for the planning committee is provided in Figure 1.3.

NEEDS ASSESSMENT ACTIVITIES

Once the planning committee—or team—has been established, it will conduct activities to determine if there is a need to create transition services in a college or community setting. A needs assessment process should be used to identify current student service needs and existing community or agency partnerships. The activities that make up this assessment process include determining the student population, identifying the number of potential students and the schools from which they may come, completing the needs assessment forms, reviewing the data, and developing a list of service changes to be made.

Form 1: Planning Committee Contact Sheet

Name	Position/Title	Organization and Address	Telephone Number	Fax Number	E-Mail Address
Donna F.	director of special education	Buckman County Public Schools Board of Education 1500 Main Street, Hansontown	555/555-2468	555/555-9874	Dflanagan@bcps.org
Marjorie M.	special education teacher	Wilson High School 104 Morning Glory Lane Hansontown	555/555-6874	555/555-8244	Mmitchell@bcps.org
Sharon W.	transition specialist	Wilson High School	555/555-4731	555/555-6873	Swhitney@bcps.org
Connie L.	principal	Wilson High School	555/555-4189	555/555-3581	Clettol.@bcps.org
Brian V.	parent	647 Broadway Hansontown	555/555-3651	555/555-4726	Bdvan@excite.com
Katie J.	transition supervisor	BCPS, BOE	555/555-4782	555/555-6911	Kjohnson2@bcps.org
Bonnie C.	case manager	State Developmental Disabilities Agency, 5448 Kentucky Ave. Edison City	555/555-8624	555/555-9247	Bclyde@statedd.gov
Brenda K.	VR counselor	State Department of Vocational Rehabilitation, 6400 Broadway Edison City	555/555-9816	555/555-6873	BrendaK@vr.gov
Frank P.	dean	Buckman County Community College, 2300 College Parkway Unionville	555/555-7325	555/555-4279	Fpinoll8184@bccc.edu

Figure 1.2. Example of a completed Form 1 for Buckman County Public Schools.

The purpose of this committee is to examine the need for new transition services for students ages 18 to 21 years with significant disabilities. Our first goal is to conduct a needs assessment during the next 3 months to review (a) the services currently provided to these students and (b) our current partnerships in the community to determine if there is a need for a new program. If the development of new services is warranted, we will create an action plan that will identify the goals and partners needed to implement these services, determine the location(s) of the services, and create a timeline for implementation. It may take 1 year or more for these services to be developed. Once the development process commences, we will meet periodically to monitor progress. Once students are receiving services, we will meet at least twice yearly as an advisory committee to discuss issues and challenges, to conduct program evaluation activities, and to review data.

Figure 1.3. Example of a planning committee mission statement.

Determine the Student Population

The purpose of determining the population of students is to limit the scope of the planning committee's activities. Although various groups of students could benefit from changes in transition services, one program cannot meet all these students' needs. The planning committee therefore must identify the particular population of students with significant disabilities who will be served. Committee members should *not* be determining the specific criteria that will eventually be used to refer students to the program. Instead, they should be identifying a group of students who may have similar needs that could be addressed by altering their current transition services. For example, School System A may want to conduct needs assessment activities based on the age of students by reviewing the current transition services for students who are 18 years or older. School System B may want to conduct assessment activities based on the type of classes or number of years students have participated in high school. Defining the population of students with significant disabilities in a school system may be a helpful first step in narrowing the focus.

The following is one example of a functional definition of *individuals with significant disabilities:* Individuals who require ongoing support in one or more major life activities to participate in an integrated community and enjoy a quality of life similar to that available to all citizens. Support may be required for life activities such as mobility, communication, self-care, and learning, as necessary for community living, employment, and self-sufficiency (TASH, 2000).

If this definition is not sufficiently descriptive or clear, committee members may choose to define *significant disabilities* in terms of a disability category, such as in the following:

Students with significant disabilities are defined as those individuals who may have a variety of disability classifications that include, but are not limited to, mental retardation, learning disabilities, traumatic brain injuries, orthopedic disabilities, autism, and behavior disorders.

Another definition of *significant disabilities* is provided in the text of the Workforce Investment Act of 1998, Title IV, Section 6, which states that the term

individual with a significant disability means an individual with a disability—
(i) who has a severe physical or mental impairment which seriously limits one or more functional capacities (such as mobility, communication, self-care, self-direction, interpersonal skills, work tolerance, or work skills) in terms of an employment outcome; (ii) whose vocational rehabilitation can be expected to require multiple vocational rehabilitation services over an extended period of time; and (iii) who has one or more physical or mental disabilities resulting from amputation, arthritis, autism, blindness, burn injury, cancer, cerebral palsy, cystic fibrosis, deafness, head injury, heart disease, hemiplegia, hemophilia, respiratory or pulmonary dysfunction, mental retardation, mental illness, multiple sclerosis, muscular dystrophy, musculoskeletal disorders, neurological disorders (including stroke and epilepsy), paraplegia, quadriplegia, and other spinal cord conditions, sickle cell anemia, specific learning disability, end-state renal disease, or another disability or combination of disabilities determined on the basis of an assessment for determining eligibility and vocational rehabilitation needs ... to cause comparable substantial functional limitation.

One other method of defining the student population is to use the type of classes in which the students currently participate, for example:

Students with significant disabilities are those who are currently participating in community-based life skills activities, who require special education support in general education classes, and are expected to require support to access and retain employment.

Once the student population has been defined, the committee will be able to determine the potential number of schools that could send students for services and, ultimately, the number of students whose needs will be assessed.

Identify the Number of Potential Students and Schools

Form 2: Potential Students and Schools (see p. 25) provides space to list the schools in the system or district that are serving the defined population of students with significant disabilities. These may include comprehensive high schools, alternative or special schools, and vocational–technical high schools. On the form is a space to list the number of older students with significant disabilities in each school. Although most programs in college or community settings are designed to serve students ages 18 to 21, we suggest including 17-year-olds in the needs assessment. Students at this age may not require transition services outside of the high school, but they may have needs that could be addressed by changing and improving services within the high school setting. An example of a completed form is provided in Figure 1.4.

Complete the Needs Assessment Forms

Included in this book are two forms that may be used to assess the current transition services and partnerships in a high school. The first is Form 3: Student Services Needs Assessment (see p. 27), which personnel can use to review the services that students are currently receiving and determine if changes are

Form 2: Potential Students and Schools

In the space provided below, list the high schools in your system that currently provide services to students ages 17 or older with significant disabilities and the approximate number of students served at each school.

High School	Number of Students 17 or Older w/ Significant Disabilities
Wilson High School	12
Corey Vocational School	6
Kennedy High School	5
Denton Center	9

Comments:

Figure 1.4. Example of a completed Form 2.

needed. A separate form should be completed for each school listed on Form 2. Members of the planning committee should complete Form 3 in conjunction with personnel in each high school who are familiar with the student population to obtain specific information about the services individual students are receiving. This form does not need to be filled out during a committee meeting. In fact, it may be best to provide copies of Form 3 to teams to take back to each school to be completed. The information collected on this form will provide the committee with an overview of transition services in each school and may also indicate programming areas that may need to be improved or enhanced. Detailed directions for completing Form 3 are provided on page 26. An example of a completed Form 3 for Wilson High School is provided in Figure 1.5.

The second part of the needs assessment process is to complete Form 4: Community Partnerships Needs Assessment (see p. 29), which identifies existing and needed school system partnerships with the community. This kind of needs assessment is sometimes referred to as *resource mapping*. The committee should examine current partnerships in terms of the resources and supports they can contribute. A separate Form 4 does not need to be completed for each high school, as long as students from all schools are served by the same agencies. This form should be completed during a committee meeting, and each committee member should bring his or her Rolodex, Palm Pilot, address book, or contact information for current partners, such as employers, community agencies serving adults, and state agencies. The purpose is to determine what resources and connections are already in place that might be used to facilitate the creation of a new program. An example of a completed Form 4 is provided in Figure 1.6. Detailed directions for completing Form 4 are provided on page 28.

Review the Needs Assessment Data

Once Forms 3 and 4 have been completed, the planning committee should convene to review the data. Remember, the purpose of the needs assessment activities is to identify current student service needs, existing and needed community or agency partnerships, changes that may be made in the current high school setting and program, and changes that would require the development of a new program in a college or community setting. The information derived from each assessment should be sufficient for the committee to determine if the creation of transition services in a college or community setting is necessary.

To make this determination, the committee should first review Form 3, going over the data in each column and deciding whether changes are needed to address students' needs. As committee members review each column, they should refer to the questions listed in Form 5: Review Questions for Student Services (see p. 30).

For example, when the committee from Wilson High School reviewed the data on the Student Services Needs Assessment (see Figure 1.5), committee members determined that changes needed to be made in four major areas: employment, inclusive experiences, extracurricular activities, and travel training. These changes are described in detail in Profile 1.1. As demonstrated in the figure and profile examples, the data may indicate that some changes could be addressed within the high school. Others would require developing new transition services in a college or community setting, especially if the high school transition services are not meeting students' needs or if there is a great deal of parental interest in service expansion.

(text continues on p. 12)

Form 3: Student Services Needs Assessment

Name of School: Wilson High School, BCPS   School Year: 2005–2006

Number of students who will receive special education services until they are 21 and who are/have:

	1	2	3	4	5		6	7		8		9	10
Age (yrs.) & # of Students	Receive SSI/SSDI	SSI/SSDI Eligible	VR Eligible	DD/MR Eligible	Included in General Education Classes	Not included in General Education Classes	Received Behavior Support	Paid Work	Unpaid Work Training	Extra-curricular Activities in School	Extracurricular Activities Outside of School	Received Travel Training	Required 1:1 Instruction
21 = 2	2	0	2	0	0	2	1	1	1	0	0	1	1
20 = 1	1	0	0	0	0	1	0	0	1	0	0	1	0
19 = 4	2	2	2	1	0	4	1	2	1	0	0	1	1
18 = 2	1	1	1	1	1	1	0	1	2	0	0	0	0
17 = 3	0	3	2	0	2	1	2	0	1	1	0	0	1
Are changes needed?					Yes	Yes	No	Yes	Yes	Yes	Yes	Yes	No

How many students or families have expressed an interest in receiving services in a college or community setting? 6

Note. SSI = Supplemental Security Income; SSDI = Social Security Disability Insurance; VR = vocational rehabilitation; DD = developmental disabilities; MR = mental retardation.

Figure 1.5. Example of a completed Form 3.

Form 4: Community Partnerships Needs Assessment

Name of Agency or Organization	Contact Person	Phone Number/ E-Mail Address	Agreement in Place	Agreement Needed or Update Needed	Changes Needed
K-Mart (Employer)	Bonnie J.	555-4848	X		
Giant Food Stores (Employer)	Daryl F.	555-8375	X		
Sunshine Retirement Village (Employer)	Cindra N.	555-8921 cnelson@aol.com	X		Update agreement to expand employment sites
PetVet (Employer)	Brad H.	555-9687 bhall@excite.com	X		
Vocational Rehabilitation Services	Karen R. Brian S.	555-9874	X		
The Arc				X	Invite to serve on planning committee
Supported Employment Enterprises				X	Need to visit, identify services
Cerebral Palsy of Buckman County				X	Visit independent living facilities
Goodwill Enterprises	John J.	555-8787	X		
Chamber of Commerce				X	Employment site?
Local Workforce Investment Board				X	Discuss potential supports
Developmental Disabilities Administration	Felicity P.	555-3254	X		
Parks and Recreation				X	Summer/after-school recreation programs
Buckman County Community College	Corey F.	555-4258 cdfosse@bccc.edu	X	Needs update	Need contact in DSS, student activities, and registration
Buckman County Police Department	Captain R.	555-5836	X		Employment site?

Figure 1.6. Example of a completed Form 4.

PROFILE 1.1
EXAMPLES OF CHANGES NEEDED AT WILSON HIGH SCHOOL

(Examples taken from data provided on Figure 1.5.)

Employment

Only one of the 17- or 18-year-old students with significant disabilities at Wilson High School has had paid work experience, and two students have not had any work experience (paid or unpaid). The committee determined that students need to be provided with more career-training activities at ages 17 and 18. This change could be addressed in the current service setting by offering students opportunities to participate in unpaid experiences in community employment settings that are already being used by the school system.

Inclusive Experiences

None of the students ages 19 to 21 years with significant disabilities are participating in any general education courses at Wilson High School. These students have no opportunity to interact with their same-age peers (because most high school students graduate at age 18); therefore, it would be difficult to address this need within the context of the high school. The committee determined that it could be addressed by accessing educational opportunities at a local community college or adult continuing education program. Courses could be audited or taken for credit in areas of interest. Developing transition services in a college or community setting might also address this need.

Extracurricular Activities

Student participation in extracurricular activities has occurred for only 1 of the 12 students assessed by the committee. The committee could address the need to develop recreational and social activities within the current program by involving students in clubs, organizations, or athletics that occur during and after school. In addition, student participation in local recreational activities outside of school could be facilitated through a partnership with the local YMCA, parks and recreation department, or other youth organizations.

Travel Training

The needs assessment in Figure 1.5 has indicated that only 3 of the 12 students have received any form of travel training. Because lack of transportation limits many aspects of life (e.g., accessing employment, recreation, or community resources), the issue of travel training needs to be addressed. Changes could be made within the current service setting by providing students with access to the county bus system or helping them learn how to call and pay for cab rides to their desired destinations. These changes might also be addressed by establishing new transition services in a community or college setting that is close to the available transportation options.

PROFILE 1.2
EXAMPLE OF PARTNERSHIP CHANGES

(Example taken from data provided on Figure 1.6.)

After completing the Community Partnerships Needs Assessment (Form 4), the Buckman County Public Schools planning committee determined that the partnership with Buckman County Community College needed to be updated. Currently, students from the high school are going to the college campus only to participate in unpaid job training situations at the bookstore. In order to meet the service needs identified on the Student Services Needs Assessment (Form 3), this partnership needs to be expanded so that students can access other college resources, such as the library, the recreation and fitness center, the career center, and computer labs. It is also possible that adult and continuing education courses offered at the college would be of interest to students. If new transition services were to be created and provided at Buckman County Community College, this agreement would have to be substantially changed.

Next, the committee should review Form 4 to determine a course of action for expanding and improving the school system's partnerships with the community. For those agencies with which the school system currently has agreements, the committee should ask the following questions:

1. Is this agreement currently being used to its fullest potential?
2. Does the agreement need to be updated?
3. If an update is needed, what changes should be made?
4. Who will contact the agency/organization to update the agreement?

For those agencies, facilities, or organizations that are not partners, the committee must ask the following questions:

1. What kind of agreement is necessary?
2. Who is the best person to obtain an agreement?
3. Do we have a contact person?
4. Could the necessary changes be addressed in the current program?
5. Do the changes require the development of a new program?
6. What contacts are already in place that could be used in the new program?
7. What other kinds of connections need to be made if a new program is to be established?

Profile 1.2 illustrates how data taken from Form 4 (see Figure 1.6) can be used to highlight the need for change in a current partnership with a local college.

Develop a List of Service Changes

As the committee reviews the data for each school, it may become evident that some systemwide changes are required, whereas other kinds of changes may need to be instituted only in a specific school. One variable members can use to determine need is the number of schools and students who would benefit. Another variable that may affect the scope of the changes is the level of interest among students and families. If families have expressed a strong interest in providing students with opportunities outside of the high school, the planning committee should consider this option carefully. Once each change area has been discussed, the planning committee will have to prioritize the list and decide whether the changes can be addressed within the current high school program or would be better accomplished in a new environment.

PLANNING NEW TRANSITION SERVICES

Once the planning committee has identified the necessary changes, the committee members must plan how and where new transition services will be provided. In this section we will review the steps involved for both the high school and college/community options.

Writing an Action Plan for High School Changes

The first activity the committee should undertake when planning new transition services is to write an action plan that addresses the changes that can be met in the high school setting. Form 6: Action Plan for High School Services (see p. 32) may be used for this purpose. Detailed directions for completing this form are provided on page 31. We suggest completing an action plan for each school; however, if most of the changes will affect all of the schools, it may be possible to create one action plan. Once the action plans are written, the committee probably will need to hold follow-up meetings to chart the progress that has been made for each goal. This will involve determining appropriate time intervals and scheduling follow-up meetings, which should be noted at the bottom of the action plan. Figure 1.7 provides an example of a completed action plan for Wilson High School. Various committee members have assumed responsibility for each action listed on the action plan (see Profile 1.3).

Once the action plan has been written, the committee should determine its next course of action. If no further changes are needed, the committee may have achieved its goals and can disband. If the needs assessment indicated that further changes require the development of new transition services outside of the high school, the planning committee will need to continue its work.

Creating New Services Outside of the High School

In the following section, we will provide an overview of the activities that would be conducted to create services in a college or community setting. These activities are identifying the focus and goals of the services, identifying potential partners, determining the location of services, setting a preliminary budget, and investigating possible funding sources.

Identify Focus and Goals of New Transition Services
The planning process may be different for each school system; however, there are some essential steps that should be conducted, the most important being to

---

Form 6: Action Plan for High School Services

Action Plan of	Buckman County	Public School System
	(fill in name of school system)	

Date Created: __10/2/05__

Name and Title	Agency
Donna F., director of special education	BCPS
Marjorie M., special education teacher	BCPS
Sharon W., transition specialist	BCPS
Brian V., parent	
Katie J., county transition supervisor	BCPS
Brenda K., counselor	Vocational Rehabilitation

Actions Needed	Person Responsible	Timeline
Provide job-training experiences for students at ages 17–18 years.	Katie J.	12/1/05
• Schedule meeting with transition personnel and job coaches.		
• Review current job tryout placements.		
• Conduct interest inventories/ situational assessments with all 17- and 18-year-olds.		
Investigate paid positions for students.	Katie J.	All year
• Conduct job development at mall.	Sharon W.	
• Meet with current training supervisors to explore possible paid positions.		11/25/05
• Contact local Workforce Investment Board.	Donna F.	11/1/05
• Contact Chamber of Commerce; get on committee.	Donna F.	11/1/05
Provide travel training on Metro bus 1x/week to all 17- to 18-year-old students. Improve partnerships with local providers of adult services.	Sharon W. Brenda K.	1/15/06
• Schedule meetings with Supported Employment Enterprises and Cerebral Palsy of B.C.	Marjorie M.	11/15/05
Facilitate participation in extracurricular activities for students ages 17–18.	Katie J.	11/1/05

Next meeting date: 12/15/05 at Wilson High School Conference Room

Figure 1.7. Example of a completed Form 6.

PROFILE 1.3
CHANGES IN THE HIGH SCHOOL

The planning committee from Buckman County Public Schools conducted a needs assessment and determined that many of the needed changes identified by the assessment could be addressed by changing the transition services currently provided in the high school. The committee decided to focus initially on four areas—employment, travel training, collaboration, and recreation—as indicated on the action plan in Figure 1.7.

To address student employment needs, the county transition supervisor and the transition specialist began arrangements to provide job-training experiences to students ages 17 and 18. They also planned to expand student opportunities for paid employment. The director of special education for the county assisted in this endeavor by agreeing to contact the local Workforce Investment Board and the Chamber of Commerce and perhaps serving on employment-related committees.

The special education teacher plans to work with the staff at her school to provide students ages 17 and 18 with travel training at least once a week. This goal will take some time to implement, and the committee has allotted 3 months for it to be initiated. The transition specialist and the vocational rehabilitation counselor plan to work together to improve partnerships with local providers of adult services and plan to schedule meetings with two local providers of supported employment. Finally, the county transition supervisor will begin to explore ways to facilitate students' participation in extracurricular activities. This action is not very detailed, and given the short timeline, it will need to be revised at the December meeting.

identify the major focus and goals of such services. The needs of the students, as identified in Form 3, should determine the focus and goals of the new transition services. For example, if a major identified need on the assessment is related to paid employment, one focus of the new transition services could be to provide paid, integrated, community employment experiences.

It is important to remember that new transition services in a college or community setting will not be able to address *all* of the identified student needs. The committee will need to prioritize the list of student needs. A good way to begin is to focus on the changes that are most essential to helping students achieve their individual transition goals. Figure 1.8 is a list—although by no means an exhaustive one—of possible service goals. The committee can use Form 7: Preliminary Goals for Service Delivery (see p. 33) to draft a list of goals. Each goal should be stated in measurable terms so that progress can be charted.

Identify Potential Partners
Based on the preliminary goals for service delivery, the committee should next determine the supports needed to achieve those goals. Using the information listed on Form 4, the committee can identify potential partners for daily operations. If representatives of these partners are not currently part of the planning committee, their involvement should be secured at this point. If various locations for providing transition services are being considered, representatives from those locations must also be contacted. Form 8: Partner Contact List (see p. 34) may be used to complete the list of partners and contacts. Figure 1.9 depicts a sample

1. To obtain employment in a full-time or part-time paid position in a job of choice in the community.

2. To participate in college classes.

3. To participate in recreational and social activities on a college campus on a regular basis.

4. To increase independent use of public transportation to access community resources.

5. To engage the support of a provider of adult services that will meet individual student needs prior to exiting public school.

6. To improve social and communication skills in community environments.

7. To develop friendships with other people of similar ages.

8. To develop age-appropriate leisure and recreation interests.

9. To access and use community resources, such as shopping centers, banks, and libraries, on a regular basis.

10. To use recreational and leisure centers in the community on a regular basis.

11. To attend and actively participate in IEP team meetings.

12. To develop and use self-advocacy skills in the areas of

    • accessing and maintaining employment,

    • arranging social engagements,

    • obtaining necessary instructional accommodations and supports in classes,

    • choosing a service provider,

    • applying for state/federal agency support (Social Security Administration, Vocational Rehabilitation, Developmental Disabilities Administration—case management).

Figure 1.8. Examples of service goals.

Partner Contact List, including the contact information for each partner and the type of partnership that the school system hopes to create. An example of a partnership created based on assessment conducted by the Buckman County Public School planning committee is provided in Profile 1.4.

Determine Location of Transition Services

Where students with significant disabilities will receive transition services depends a great deal on the identified goals. If the focus will be on community employment and travel training, services in a community employment location close to public transportation may be the best choice. If the focus will be on increasing students' opportunities for participating in classes and recreational activities with peers without disabilities, a community college or university setting would be optimal.

All transition services do not need to be provided in one location. One site may be chosen as a central setting in which students will be served, but they may participate in instructional, employment, and recreational activities in other college

Form 8: Partner Contact List

Name of Agency or Organization	Contact Person	Phone Number/ E-Mail Address	Committee Member Who Will Make Contact	Type of Partnership
K-Mart	Bonnie J.	555-4848	Donna F.	Employment
Giant Food Stores	Daryl F.	555-8375	Marjorie M.	Employment
Sunshine Retirement Village	Cindra N.	555-8921 cnelson@aol.com	Sharon W.	Employment
PetVet	Brad H.	555-9687 bhall@excite.com	Connie L.	Employment
Vocational Rehabilitation Services	Karen R. Brian S.	555-9874	Brian V.	Committee: Job Coaching Instruction
The Arc			Katie J.	Committee: Instruction
Supported Employment Enterprises			Sharon W.	Committee: Job Coaching Instruction
Cerebral Palsy of Buckman County			Katie J.	Committee: Instruction
Goodwill Enterprises	John J.	555-8787	Sharon W.	Committee: Instruction
Chamber of Commerce			Donna F.	Committee: Instruction
Local Workforce Investment Board			Katie J.	Committee: Employment
Developmental Disabilities Administration	Felicity P.	555-3254	Katie J.	Committee: Instruction
Buckman County Community College	Corey F.	555-4258 cdfosse@bccc.edu	Sharon W.	Committee: Instruction
Parks and Recreation				Training Access
State University			Donna F.	Committee: Instruction
Buckman County Police Department	Captain R.	555-5836	Donna F.	Employment

Figure 1.9. Example of a completed Form 8.

PROFILE 1.4
PARTNERSHIP WITH SUPPORTED EMPLOYMENT ENTERPRISES

The Community Partnerships Needs Assessment (Form 4) conducted by the Buckman County Public Schools (BCPS) planning committee identified that no current agreement existed between BCPS and one of the region's largest providers of employment services, Supported Employment Enterprises, Inc. (SEE). The committee hopes to create an agreement with this organization that will include a number of activities. First, committee members would like to engage someone from SEE to serve on the planning committee. If possible, the committee would also like to see if the agency would be able to provide some assistance with job coaching services for students. Finally, BCPS hopes that someone from SEE will provide instruction to students in the areas of résumé building, interviewing, and job-keeping skills. The transition specialist, Sharon W., is in charge of contacting SEE and facilitating the development of an agreement to address each of these areas. Once an agreement is created, Sharon would update the Partner Contact List (Form 8) with the name and telephone number or e-mail address (or both) of the SEE contact person so that involved personnel would know whom to contact at that agency.

or community settings. For example, services may be centrally located in a community recreation center such as a YMCA; however, students may attend classes and use other facilities at the local community college.

The impetus for creating transition services in a college or community setting is to provide students with significant disabilities with access to *integrated experiences* that will help them move from school to adult life. When considering possible locations, committee members must keep in mind the need for these types of experiences. Establishing services in a setting in which students are isolated for all or part of their days must be avoided. We will now describe some of the pros and cons of various college or community locations. A summary of these pros and cons is provided in Figure 1.10.

Pros and cons of 4-year college/university location. Transition services based at 4-year colleges provide many opportunities for integrated experiences for students with significant disabilities. These institutions generally have departments in the social sciences and medical fields, such as education; social work; psychology; and speech, occupational, and physical therapies. College students majoring in these areas often need formal and informal experiences involving students with disabilities. Partnerships can be developed with the staff in these departments that will serve both the students with significant disabilities and the college students. For example, they may work with one another in classes, practica experiences, and student service–learning experiences. Four-year institutions are typically larger than community colleges and often provide housing for college students, which affords students with significant disabilities greater access to college-age peers during the daytime, evenings, and weekends than does a community college. Unfortunately, the admissions and application requirements of 4-year schools—along with tuition costs—may prove difficult to overcome when trying to gain access to this postsecondary setting. Finally, individuals who

Pros	Cons
Four-Year College/University	
Wide array of coursework	Less prevalent
Many clubs/organizations	Admissions & application process
Social sciences/medical departments	Tuition
Stable student population	Attitudinal barriers
Residential possibilities	
Community College	
Open-door policies	Transient student population
Nontraditional students	Limited access to potential peer support
Proximity	Space may be limited
Fellow graduates as peers	Attitudinal barriers
Lower costs (tuition waived)	
Community Settings	
Natural setting for students not going to college	Lack of access to same-age peers
Access to employment and CBI sites	May lead to segregated experiences
Daily living or social activities	Transportation barriers
Doesn't preclude possible college connections	

Figure 1.10. Location pros and cons.

are interested in providing transition services to students with significant disabilities at a 4-year college or university should be prepared to encounter some attitudinal barriers posed by faculty and staff members who may not understand the purpose of serving students with significant disabilities on a college campus.

Pros and cons of community college location. Community colleges are also attractive locations for services because they often have open-door policies that may facilitate access for nontraditional students. In addition, these facilities are more prevalent than 4-year institutions. A community college is often the first postsecondary experience for individuals exiting high school, and it is a good setting for integrated experiences. The students who attend community colleges are often very transient, however; they come to campus each day to attend classes and leave it soon after. When residential services are not available, students who commute to a community college may not spend a great deal of "down time" there. This may decrease the number of opportunities for college students to serve as peer buddies and may limit social interactions and participation in campus clubs and organizations for the students with disabilities. In addition, securing office and classroom space in a community college can be difficult, and, as with 4-year schools, faculty and staff members may present attitudinal barriers.

Pros and cons of community settings. Transition services may be provided in various community locations, such as employment sites, recreational facilities, residential settings (e.g., apartment or house), or in government offices. At first, these places may not seem like ideal locations, but planning committees should not overlook the possible benefits of such sites. Business environments often do not have the same space concerns as college campuses. In addition, basing transition services in a community location does not preclude students from enrolling in college classes or participating in recreational and social activities on campuses or in other community settings. Students with disabilities are able to go to and from the campus to participate in these activities in the same way other college students would. Basing a program in a community location may also increase employment opportunities. Care must be taken to ensure that students with significant disabilities are provided with integrated experiences if transition services are based in the community. Profile 1.5 offers examples of programs that successfully provide transition services in community settings.

Other considerations. Once the planning committee has determined which type of setting would best meet students' needs, other considerations should be taken into account prior to choosing a final location. These considerations are listed in Form 9: Location Checklist (see p. 35). Committee members should review the questions on this form and add any other considerations that pertain to meeting student or staff needs in a particular location. Examples include contacts, time, other users, costs, office space, accessibility, resources, location, and access to peers.

Set a Preliminary Budget
When the planning committee has chosen a location, committee members can begin to create a preliminary program budget based on the number of students to be served. Funding and resources may come from the school system or may be contributed by a partner (e.g., vocational rehabilitation facilities, employers, providers serving adults, local One Stop centers). Committee members should make note of potential partners or other contributors who may be able to provide resources or services free of charge. Form 10: Preliminary Budget (see p. 36) may be used to set a preliminary budget for the program.

Investigate Funding Sources
With a preliminary budget established, the planning committee can now review the various costs of providing transition services in a college or community setting and determine if additional funds must be obtained before program implementation begins. It is important to keep in mind that the fiscal year for many school systems begins July 1 and that most school systems need to have estimated program costs included in the budget at least 1 year prior to actual implementation. Possible funding sources are listed in Figure 1.11.

PROFILE 1.5
EXAMPLES OF TRANSITION SERVICES IN COMMUNITY SETTINGS

1. The Adult Independence Program in Charles County, Maryland, is an example of how transition services can be successfully provided in a community setting. This program is located in the Towne Center Mall, where it shares space with the sheriff's office. Through a collaborative agreement, the students use the sheriff's office for independent instruction, and the program teachers have office space there. Two special education teachers and two paraprofessionals support 18 students in this program. Job coaching on an as-needed basis is provided by school system personnel and private vendors. Students have opportunities to access other postsecondary environments—including the local community college—to take noncredit courses, work in the community, and participate in college recreation or club activities.

2. The ACCESS Program, which is located in a house in Overland Park, Kansas, is a second example. Two special education teachers, one occupational therapist, and a part-time transition specialist work with 30 students. On any given day, students participate in classes (math, newsletter, social skills, sports activities), exercise at the Jewish Community Center (JCC) athletic center and work on expanding reading and math skills at the JCC achievement center, and work at a job in the community.

3. LifeLink uses an apartment as a setting for its transition services in State College, Pennsylvania. Three teachers, one supervisor, and seven to nine job coaches support 45 to 55 students. In concept, LifeLink functions much like a science or computer lab, where students can learn transition skills. Groups of students requiring transition education determine their skills and needs, set goals, and then schedule the LifeLink Lab, a living classroom. While still in high school, the students take turns living in the apartment with a transition coach, who oversees their stays and helps teach various life skills. Students begin by staying in the apartment for short periods of time and lengthen their stays as they adjust to independent living. The program has been expanded to include a second apartment. The transition coaches do not live with the students in this apartment, but reside in an apartment nearby. The students thus make the last step in the transition to independent living, living on their own with little or no supervision.

Note. Descriptions retrieved from the Transition Coalition database of Community-Based Special Education Programs: http://www.ku.edu/cgiwrap/tcacs/spedprograms/search/index.php

- **Federal government agencies,** such as the Department of Education, provide a number of different funding programs. For example, the Department of Education offers programs through the Office of Special Education and Rehabilitative Services (OSERS) that could be used to fund a new program. Go to http://www.ed.gov/about/offices/list/OSERS/index.html and select "grants and funding" to review the available grants.

- **State departments of education, developmental disabilities councils, or Workforce Investment Boards** may have funds (discretionary grant funds, state improvement grant funds, innovative projects) that could be obtained through grant proposals used to improve or expand services in local school systems. Contact your local state offices to determine if funds are available and how to apply for them.

- **National corporations and foundations** offer grants to improve educational services to students with disabilities. In addition, local businesses may be willing to donate resources or space needed to implement a program.

- **Fees for services or tuition** may be sought from other school systems that would like to send a student to your program. If your school system does not have a constant or large population of students who will need the services provided by the new program, and it decides to accept students from nearby systems, it may be possible to charge those systems a fee for services.

- **Fund-raising events or activities** may be held if the program requires particular pieces of equipment (e.g., computers, assistive technology, office equipment). Consider involving students, families, and staff members in fund-raising activities. These types of activities can also be used to generate funds for particular student activities once the program commences.

Figure 1.11. Potential funding sources.

Chapter 1
Reproducible Forms

Form 1: Planning Committee Contact Sheet

Name	Position/Title	Organization and Address	Telephone Number	Fax Number	E-Mail Address

Form 2: Potential Students and Schools

In the space provided below, list the high schools in your system that currently provide services to students ages 17 or older with significant disabilities and the approximate number of students served at each school.

High School

Number of Students 17 or Older w/ Significant Disabilities

_____   _____

_____   _____

_____   _____

_____   _____

_____   _____

_____   _____

_____   _____

_____   _____

_____   _____

_____   _____

_____   _____

_____   _____

_____   _____

_____   _____

Comments:

Directions for Completing Form 3:
Student Services Needs Assessment

1. Identify the sending school and school year at the top of the form.

2. In column 1, write the number of students from the school who are in each age bracket listed.

3. In column 2, write the number of students who are currently receiving, or are eligible to receive, Supplemental Security Income or Social Security Disability Insurance from the Social Security Administration. Eligibility status may be one of the characteristics used during the referral process to describe a student. In addition, school personnel can determine if students who may be eligible have completed the necessary paperwork.

4. In column 3, write the number of students who may be eligible to receive services from your state vocational rehabilitation office. If a student may be eligible but has not yet applied for such services, high school personnel should address this issue.

5. In column 4, write the number of students who may be eligible to receive services from your state developmental disabilities case management agency (Office of Mental Retardation or Developmental Disabilities Administration). If a student may be eligible but has not yet applied for these services, high school personnel should address this issue.

6. In column 5, write the number of students who have and have not participated in general education classes. This will help determine the extent to which students in this school have had inclusive experiences and will facilitate the discussion regarding students' need for expanded opportunities in this area.

7. In column 6, write the number of students who have a behavior support plan. Students' behaviors may affect their referral status.

8. In column 7, write the number of students in each age group who have had paid and unpaid employment experiences. This will provide a summary of the students' vocational experiences, clarify how these experiences differ by age group, and highlight potential areas for changes in vocational services.

9. In column 8, write the number of students who have participated in extracurricular activities both in and outside of school. This information may be used to identify student activities of interest that could be expanded or enhanced in a new or updated program. In addition, participation in extracurricular activities is often overlooked in transition programs and could be addressed in a college or community setting.

10. In column 9, write the number of students who have received travel training, which gives students access to employment and to community resources and recreational facilities. If travel training has not been emphasized in the high school, this change could be made either in the high school or in the new transition program.

11. In column 10, write the number of students in each age range who require one-on-one assistance. This will pinpoint the amount and types of support the students require and may also indicate a future personnel issue.

12. At the bottom of the form, write the number of students or families who have expressed an interest in receiving services outside of the high school. This often is one of the most critical factors in developing new transition services.

Form 3: Student Services Needs Assessment

Name of School: _____

School Year: _____

Number of students who will receive special education services until they are 21 and who are/have:

Age (yrs.) & # of Students	1 Receive SSI/SSDI	2 SSI/SSDI Eligible	3 VR Eligible	4 DD/MR Eligible	5 Included in General Education Classes	5 Not included in General Education Classes	6 Received Behavior Support	Paid Work	7 Unpaid Work Training	Extra-curricular Activities in School	8 Extracurricular Activities Outside of School	9 Received Travel Training	10 Required 1:1 Instruction
21 =													
20 =													
19 =													
18 =													
17 =													
Are changes needed?													

How many students or families have expressed an interest in receiving services in a college or community setting? _____

Note. SSI = Supplemental Security Income; SSDI = Social Security Disability Insurance; VR = vocational rehabilitation; DD = developmental disabilities; MR = mental retardation.

Directions for Completing Form 4:
Community Partnerships Needs Assessment

1. In column 1, write the names of persons or organizations (e.g., YMCA, The Arc) in your community that have collaborative agreements with the school system. Also fill in the names of other agencies, facilities, or organizations that could potentially provide services, access to employment or instructional settings, or support to students.

2. In column 2, write the name (or names) of the contact person(s) at each agency, facility, or organization.

3. In column 3, write the phone number or e-mail address (or both) for each contact person.

4. Check column 4 if an agreement currently exists.

5. Check column 5 if an agreement needs to be established or updated.

6. In column 6, write the changes needed for each listing. For example, if an agreement does not currently exist, changes could include scheduling a meeting with a representative of that agency or organization to discuss potential partnerships, making new contacts, or inviting a representative to a planning committee meeting.

Form 4: Community Partnerships Needs Assessment

Name of Agency or Organization	Contact Person	Phone Number/ E-Mail Address	Agreement in Place	Agreement Needed or Update Needed	Changes Needed

Form 5: Review Questions for Student Services

1. Are changes needed only for a particular age group (e.g., 17- to 18-year-olds) or for all students?

2. What kinds of changes are needed?

3. Does the issue of student application for Supplemental Security Income, vocational rehabilitation, or developmental disability services or supports need to be addressed by current school personnel?

4. Does the amount of self-contained instruction for students need to be changed?

5. Does the frequency or variety of inclusive experiences need to be increased?

6. Should more students have paid jobs?

7. Do students need more opportunities to participate in recreational or extracurricular activities with their peers?

8. How could the frequency of participation in recreational or extracurricular activities and level of independence for students be improved by increasing their travel training?

9. Could the changes identified in Questions 1 through 8 be addressed in the current location?

10. Do the changes identified in Questions 1 through 8 require the development of new services in a college or community setting?

11. How will services in a college or community setting be different from what is currently available?

12. What setting is best equipped to meet students' needs?

Directions for Completing Form 6:
Action Plan for High School Services

1. Write the name of the school system at the top of the action plan.

2. Indicate the date the action plan was written.

3. Have each member of the committee who is involved in designing the action plan write his or her name, position, and the agency for which he or she works. Any member who is not present at this meeting should not be deemed responsible for any of the actions on the plan.

4. Reiterate the changes needed in the high school identified through review of the needs assessment data.

5. List the actions that must be taken to meet these needs.

6. Designate a person who will be responsible for completing these actions.

7. Create a timeline in which the actions will take place.

8. Determine the date and place for a follow-up meeting at which the committee will review progress toward implementing this action plan.

Form 6: Action Plan for High School Services

Action Plan of _____ Public School System
(fill in name of school system)

Date Created: _____

Name and Title

_____

_____

_____

_____

_____

Agency

_____

_____

_____

_____

Actions Needed	Person Responsible	Timeline

Next meeting date:

Form 7: Preliminary Goals for Service Delivery

Date of Meeting:

Meeting Attended By:

1. _____

2. _____

3. _____

4. _____

5. _____

6. _____

7. _____

8. _____

9. _____

10. _____

Comments:

Form 8: Partner Contact List

Name of Agency or Organization	Contact Person	Phone Number/ E-Mail Address	Committee Member Who Will Make Contact	Type of Partnership

Form 9: Location Checklist

Contacts

Do you have any personal connections who could help you obtain space? The best people to engage are those in administrative positions (e.g., president, manager, CEO, dean, provost, department chair).

Time

When is space available?
Will the availability correspond with a school day/year schedule?

Other Users

Is this location currently being used by other persons or groups in the school system or by other school systems to provide job experiences or community-based instruction?

Costs

Does the space have to be leased, or can it be donated or bartered for?

Office Space

Is there access to desks, phones, computers, a fax machine, and a copier?

Accessibility

Is it close to public transportation or on a bus line connecting with the school?

Resources

Is it near (a) facilities and businesses that you plan to use for instruction or employment, such as restaurants, banks, post offices, shopping centers, colleges, and libraries, and (b) sites for social/extracurricular activities, such as the YMCA or a community recreation center?

Location

If a college site, what other services are close to the specific building to be used (e.g., cafeteria, student lounge, health center, post office, computer room, career center, bookstore, library, other departments)?

Access to Peers

Does the location offer opportunities for the students with disabilities to interact with their peers who are nondisabled in structured and unstructured activities?

Other:

Form 10: Preliminary Budget

Item	Cost	LSS Funded	Contributed	Potential Contributor(s)
Staff				
Teacher				
Transition support				
Paraprofessional(s)				
Adjunct college staff				
Providers of adult services				
Equipment/Materials				
Computer equipment				
Telephone				
Cell phone				
Pager				
Copying/fax costs				
Internet/e-mail access				
Storage equipment(e.g., filing cabinets, locked closets)				
Curriculum				
Desks				
Chairs				
Other				
Rental of space				
Transportation				
Tuition for classes				
Possible student work supplies (e.g., wardrobe)				

Note. LSS = local school system.

CHAPTER 2
Implementation

Moving from planning to implementing new transition services requires that logistics be addressed. Although student services will be individualized, the policies and procedures of these new services must be clearly established. This will create an infrastructure to support the continued provision of services and will ensure that they are implemented consistently from year to year. The second element of implementation is determining how services will be provided on a daily basis. One of the most exciting aspects of serving students with significant disabilities outside of the high school is the wide array of learning environments and opportunities it affords them. These expanded opportunities also mean that coordinating student activities and schedules will be challenging. Organization and documentation of student and staff activities will both become essential elements of making things work.

Flexibility and adaptation are crucial to success. No matter how well the planning process was conducted, unexpected pitfalls and unforeseen challenges will arise. Having realistic expectations about the amount of time that it will take to implement new transition services is essential because implementation will almost certainly take longer than initially expected. Try to be patient with those individuals who continue to be challenged by the vision being created. Most important, time must be allotted for building relationships with the partners who are involved in this process and the students who are being served. True changes in student experiences and outcomes will be created through these relationships.

POLICIES AND PROCEDURES

As noted previously, ensuring the successful implementation of new transition services in a college or community setting requires putting in place policies and procedures to provide structure for the staff and students. There are seven steps in this process:

1. creating an overview of services,
2. hiring the necessary staff,
3. creating application and referral procedures,
4. developing a transportation plan,
5. finalizing the budget and funding sources,
6. drawing up written agreements with collaborators, and
7. setting policies for services.

Each of these activities will be reviewed in this section.

Create an Overview

Prior to implementation, the planning committee should create a written overview describing the services that will be provided in the college or community setting. This overview should include a description of the students who would most benefit, the goals and outcomes for participating students, a proposed timeline for implementation, the partners, a description of costs and contributions, student insurance coverage (for questions pertaining to liability), the staff-to-student ratio in classroom and community, how services will differ from those provided in the high school, and the evaluation measures. This overview will be provided to local school system administrators, potential community partners, college personnel, and families. The committee may designate a person who will coordinate completion of this document using Form 11: Overview (see p. 64). Profile 2.1 demonstrates how the fictional Buckman County planning team used this form to write an overview of their new transition services.

Hire Staff

Once the committee has written and disseminated the overview, the next task is to inform the local school system about the staff who will need to be hired or reassigned to provide the new transition services. Based upon the number of students to be served, the committee should make recommendations about the number and types of staff that will be required. This list should include a coordinator, paraprofessionals, full- or part-time transition personnel, and job coaches. In making this recommendation, the committee should maintain a balance between a necessary level of supervision and the increased level of independence expected of students in a college or community setting. Staff-to-student ratios must be low enough to ensure that community-based instructional activities can be conducted in small groups or individually.

Candidates for these staff positions should be certified secondary special educators who have experience in job placement and community-based instruction. Ideally, the paraprofessionals will also have had experience supporting students with significant disabilities outside of the classroom. If job candidates do not have this experience, the committee should determine how to provide new hires with additional training before they begin to work with students. It may also be beneficial to identify potential staff members from outside agencies with whom the staff may consult or whom they may enlist to serve as guest instructors. All staff members should be provided with business cards and e-mail accounts, as these will assist in projecting a professional image in the higher education and business communities.

Create Application and Referral Procedures

Create Student Profile

Using the information compiled on Form 3: Student Services Needs Assessment, in Chapter 1, the committee should be able to create a profile of the students with significant disabilities who would most likely benefit from new transition services in a college or community setting. This profile could include characteristics such as age, years in the school system, eligibility for Supplemental Security

PROFILE 2.1

OVERVIEW OF TRANSITION SERVICES DEVELOPED BY BUCKMAN COUNTY PUBLIC SCHOOLS

Description

These transition services are designed to meet the needs of students with cognitive disabilities who attend public school until age 21 and will graduate with a high school certificate. Students will already have spent at least 4 years in a high school, and they may receive services at the college for 1 to 3 years. The focus of services will emphasize learning communication, decision-making, interpersonal, personal management, career or vocational, and recreation or leisure skills in integrated college and community settings. The services will be based at the local community college; however, students may receive instruction not only on the college campus but also in the community and at their employment sites. Students will have the opportunity to attend classes of their choice at the college, and they will be placed in paid employment, according to their skills and interests. The remainder of the student's day will be spent in work settings or recreation or leisure environments in the community. The amount of time each student may spend in any environment will be determined by his or her specific needs.

Staffing

Up to 10 students will be served, with one full-time coordinator and two full-time instructional assistants working as job and educational coaches.

Liability

Students are covered under the school system's insurance policy under the same provisions as they would be during any instructional activity conducted in the community.

Facilities

The location will be Room 102 of the student union at Buckman County Community College. Students will have access to one designated classroom for 1.5 hours in the morning and 1.5 hours in the afternoon. Student may use all campus facilities, including the library, recreational center, career center, cafeteria, and bookstore. The instructional staff will have access to an office, which will be supplied by the college, with a desk, bookcase, Internet access, and phone service. The local school system will provide the staff with a computer, fax machine, filing cabinets, and curricula. Copying costs will be charged to the local school system on a monthly basis.

Collaborators

Collaborative partners will include staff from Buckman County Community College, local service providers in the community (as listed on the partner contact sheet), and the Office of Vocational Rehabilitation.

(continues)

PROFILE 2.1
Continued.

Transportation

Transportation will be provided to and from the college site by the local school system; however, travel training will be provided to those students who have accessible public transportation, and they will be expected to use it.

Outcomes

Upon completion, students will have accomplished the following:

1. completed the requirements for a high school certificate;
2. attended and actively participated in their IEP team meetings;
3. developed and used self-advocacy skills in the areas of accessing employment, arranging social engagements, and choosing a service provider;
4. participated in one college course of their choice per year;
5. participated in a variety of work experiences resulting in paid employment;
6. used community resources, such as shopping centers, banks, and libraries;
7. participated in and used recreational or leisure centers in the community on a regular basis; and
8. accessed and used public transportation for traveling with and without support.

Timeline

Planning will begin in August of 2005. Implementation is scheduled for September of 2006.

Program Evaluation

The program will be evaluated twice yearly via student and family satisfaction surveys. Follow-up with graduates will be conducted for 3 to 5 years.

Income, work experiences, or community experiences. A list of potential characteristics that could be used in a student profile is provided in Figure 2.1. This list is not exhaustive, and there may be other characteristics that should be considered in a particular school system.

Establish Referral Protocol

A referral protocol is a step-by-step guide that details the process through which all students will be referred for new services. In addition to the referral procedures, the protocol should specify the types of documentation that will be needed to support a student's referral. A checklist of these documents, including the student's Individualized Education Program (IEP), team notes, career portfolio, current assessments, and other objective data providing information about the student's previous experiences, should be a part of the referral protocol given to referring teachers.

BUCKMAN COUNTY PUBLIC SCHOOLS
STUDENT PROFILE

Please review this profile when making referral decisions for your students for transition services at Buckman County Community College. If you have questions regarding a particular student, please contact Arlene D., Area Transition Supervisor, at 555-1234 or adgastino@nrbcps.nostate.us

Students who are successfully receiving transition services at Buckman County Community College:

☐ Have a developmental disability

☐ Have completed 4 years of high school

☐ Will not receive a standard high school diploma

☐ Will complete the state's alternative assessment

☐ Are eligible for or are receiving SSI

☐ Can travel independently or be instructed in the use of public transportation

☐ Have had two paid or unpaid community work experiences

☐ Can exhibit socially responsible behavior when left unsupervised

☐ Are able to communicate with others

☐ Are able to perform basic personal care functions

☐ Are between the ages of 18 and 21 years

☐ Have satisfactory school attendance

☐ Have a desire to receive transition services outside of the high school

☐ Have exhibited a need and desire for greater independence

☐ Have not had any disciplinary action in the past 2 years

Figure 2.1. Example of a student profile.

This protocol must be distributed and explained to all possible referring personnel prior to any referrals being made. In addition, the protocol should clearly state the person to whom all questions or disputes about referrals should be made, such as a supervisor or director. Figure 2.2 provides an example of the referral protocol created by the fictional Buckman County Public Schools.

Develop Student Application
Creating an application for services may be useful in the referral process in a variety of ways. First, an application may provide important information about a student's previous school and community experiences. In addition, the application can be used to assess student and parent interest and provide students with a means of communicating their expectations. Finally, an application underscores the differences between the high school and the new transition services

BUCKMAN COUNTY PUBLIC SCHOOLS
TRANSITION SERVICES AT BUCKMAN COUNTY
COMMUNITY COLLEGE REFERRAL PROTOCOL

Please complete the following steps when referring students for services at Buckman County Community College. If you have questions regarding a particular referral, please contact Arlene D., Area Transition Supervisor, at 555-1234, or adgastino@nrbcps.nostate.us

1. Review overview, including the goals and objectives.

2. Review caseload to determine students who may benefit.

3. Review student profile (attached).

4. Review student records to create a list of potential students.

5. Compile referral documentation, including the following:

   - Copy of IEP
   - Team notes from last IEP meeting
   - Copy of current educational and psychological assessments
   - Results of interest inventories
   - Functional skills inventory
   - Summary of inclusive experiences
   - Summary of previous vocational experiences, paid and unpaid
   - Student résumé or career portfolio
   - Previous experience with public transportation
   - Description of mobility and transportation skills
   - Student-centered planning
   - Other:

6. Contact area supervisor to discuss potential referrals.

After meeting with the area supervisor, the following steps will be taken:

1. The coordinator will be invited to the IEP meeting of students who may be referred.

2. The student and his or her parents will be contacted to determine the level of interest.

3. A visit to the college will be scheduled for the student and his or her family to observe the environment and the corresponding increased expectations.

4. The coordinator and area supervisor will meet with the parents and student to discuss questions, concerns, and fears related to receiving transition services at the college.

5. If interested, the student will complete an application.

6. The decision to refer a student will ultimately be made at the student's IEP meeting by parents, student, and school system personnel.

Figure 2.2. Example of a referral protocol.

and establishes at the outset that students will be expected to become more involved in their education. Form 12: Student Application (see p. 65) may be used as a template.

Determine Methods of Dissemination

Once the committee has created the referral and application procedures, it must determine how this information will be supplied to interested parties. One method is to create a brochure for distribution to teachers, parents, and students. It might also be helpful to schedule meetings with high school teachers and administrators who have not been involved in the planning to inform them of the purpose of the new transition services and to familiarize them with the referral protocol. A meeting will also give local school system personnel an opportunity to ask questions about the students who might be served and how the referral and application process will work. Information about the new transition services can be provided to parents and students by including it in a school newsletter; listing it on the school system Web site; or distributing it during open houses, at back-to-school nights, or at IEP meetings.

Develop a Transportation Plan

Another important issue that the committee will have to address during implementation is that of transportation. Learning how to travel independently to a college or other community location is an age-appropriate and extremely vital skill for students with significant disabilities to acquire. The committee will need to determine when transportation will be provided by the school system, the routes that will be used—or if there is a need to establish new routes—and how the costs will be managed. If the school system is in an urban setting, some students may be able to use public transportation to get to and from the college or community setting or to and from their job sites. Some school systems require students to participate in travel training so that ultimately they can independently travel to and from the college or community setting. Other school systems have required that students provide their own transportation. The committee might consider inviting someone familiar with both the local school system and public transportation routes to the meetings in which a transportation plan is developed. Form 13: Transportation Plan Checklist (see p. 71) will help to guide the development of this plan.

Finalize the Budget and Funding Sources

Using the preliminary budget established on Form 10: Preliminary Budget, in Chapter 1 (see p. 36), the committee can finalize the approximate cost of services and determine which funding sources will be used. This is a good time to establish the means through which the coordinator and staff members will access the budget. For example, will staff members have to obtain supplies and materials through a nearby high school, or will they have their own source? The budget for the first year should address start-up costs, such as creating brochures, purchasing curricula and materials, and obtaining equipment such as computers and furniture (e.g., locking filing cabinet, storage closet). When anticipating costs for the following year, the committee should try to determine if the number of students will increase, thereby creating a need for additional staff. This information should be presented to the local school system administration as early as possible so that appropriate allocations can be made in the school's budget.

Draw Up Written Agreements

Written agreements between the local school system and those organizations involved in providing resources, services, or supports to students should be created. Form 14: Written Agreement (see p. 73) may be used for this purpose. These agreements may be between the local school system and the college or community site at which the students will participate. Agreements also may be made between the local school system and individuals, such as adult service personnel in the community or adjunct faculty members, who have agreed to provide instruction or serve as guest speakers. To determine the number and kind of agreements that need to be created or established, the committee should review the community partnerships listed on Form 4: Community Partnerships Needs Assessment, in Chapter 1 (see p. 29). Written agreements (sometimes called "Memorandums of Understanding," or MOUs) should include various elements, such as designation of a point person or liaison at the postsecondary site, the time frame, insurance, use of resources (classroom, computer lab, recreational facilities), and a termination clause (the terms under which the agreement may be terminated). The committee should determine where all agreements will be filed and provide the coordinator with copies, because he or she will need to be familiar with the terms of all agreements. Figure 2.3 is a sample agreement between a local school system and a local community college.

Set Policies

Implementing transition services in a college or community setting creates the need for a variety of new policies. To avoid confusion, the committee should address topics such as graduation, record keeping and finances, administration, waivers, free and reduced lunches, emergency procedures, and scheduling prior to implementing services. Form 15: Policy Checklist (see p. 75) lists questions that may be used to facilitate this discussion and guide the creation of these new policies. Once established, policies should be recorded and copies should be provided to appropriate staff members and administrators.

Form 14: Written Agreement

Between _____Buckman County Public_____ and _____Buckman County Community College_____
(school or school system)

This AGREEMENT, made on ___9/27/05___ by and between the _____Buckman County Public Schools (BCPS)_____
(date)   (name of school or school system)

Board of Education __14141 School Drive, Buckman County__ and the _____Buckman County Community College (BCCC)_____
(address)   (name of institution or organization)

_____9898 College Avenue, Buckman County_____, hereby follows:
(address)

1. Scope of Services

The Board of Education will provide transition services for individuals with developmental disabilities at this location at BCCC. Up to 14 individuals ages 18 to 21 years who continue to need special education and who have continuing needs for transition, as evidenced by the Individualized Education Program (IEP), will be considered for this placement. Students will be accepted for services through an application process matching each student's learning outcomes as established by the IEP to the services provided at this location.

2. Duties of the BCPS Board

The Board's obligations and duties under this agreement shall be as follows:

(a) The Board shall provide one special education instructor/coordinator to be present at the Institution.

(b) The Board shall provide staff support as determined by the students' needs.

(c) The Board shall be responsible for any costs associated with services, including—but not limited to—materials and equipment, transportation, and incidental costs.

(d) The Board agrees to provide school bus transportation to and from the Institution and each student's home.

(e) Incidental costs (e.g., photocopier, fax, telephone) will be paid by the Board upon receipt of invoice.

(f) If the students seek enrollment in the Institution's credit or noncredit classes, these students will meet all admissions requirements, academic requirements, and all other policies related to enrolling and participating in classes.

(g) The Board's instructor will familiarize him- or herself with the Institution's code of conduct, relate these standards to other Board staff and students, and assume responsibility for enforcing and abiding by these standards.

3. Duties of the Institution

The Institution's obligations and duties under this agreement shall be as follows:

(a) The Institution shall permit the Board to explore and use its facilities for educational purposes.

(continues)

Figure 2.3. Example of a completed Form 14 for a school system and a community college.

(b) The Institution shall provide one classroom for use by the Board available from {time} to {time}, Monday through Friday, during the academic year.

(c) The Institution shall provide one office area for exclusive use by the Board during the academic year.

(d) The Institution shall provide the Board with a telephone and computer for the Board's use, pursuant to Section 4 below.

(e) The Institution shall permit the Board to have access to Institution faculty or staff members who have agreed to assist the Board in developing educational services for Board students, as well as to Institution student interns who may wish to collaborate with or support students.

(f) The Institution shall provide the Board with information and access to employment opportunities at the Institution for Board students.

4. Fees

The Board agrees to pay the Institution rent, which includes a monthly telephone connection. In addition, the Board agrees to pay for all telephone calls made from the Institution. The charges will be as follows:

• Rental for office and classroom space shall be at the rate of $300.00 per month, invoiced to the Board at the beginning of the semester or the effective date of this agreement, whichever is later, and due within thirty (30) days of invoice.

• Local calls shall be billed at the cost of $.10 for the first minute and $.06 for each additional minute. Long-distance calls shall be billed at a cost of $.20 per minute. Telephone charges shall be invoiced to the Board on a monthly basis and shall be due within thirty (30) days of invoice.

5. Liability Insurance and Indemnification

• The Board agrees that its property and liability insurance coverage shall include the premises utilized by the Board staff and students at the Institution.

• The Board agrees to indemnify and hold harmless and defend (at the election of the Institution) the State of Maryland and the Institution—and their agents, employees, and officers—with respect to any and all liability, including any claims, costs or expenses, damages, judgments, actions, or causes of action arising directly or indirectly at any time during or after the term of this agreement, and which are caused in whole or in part from the action or inaction of the Board's agents, employees, faculty, or invitees.

6. Term and Termination

The effective date of this agreement shall be 10/1/05, and this agreement shall terminate on 5/25/06. At the conclusion of this agreement, the Institution and the Board shall collaborate to determine whether to continue this agreement.

Signatures and Titles

_____   _____

_____   _____

_____   _____

Figure 2.3. *Continued.*

DAILY OPERATIONS

Once the committee has created the policies and procedures, the next step is to prepare for daily operations. Although the committee will continue to be a part of the activities, the new staff, and most important, the coordinator, will need to be involved in planning for daily operations. Seven steps will help in preparing for daily operations:

1. researching the protocol and procedures of the new setting,
2. identifying inclusive opportunities for students,
3. determining educational environments and staffing,
4. determining student goals,
5. purchasing or developing curricula,
6. developing weekly schedules and individual student schedules, and
7. monitoring staff and student activities.

Research Protocol and Procedures of New Setting

Providing transition services outside the high school means operating under a whole new set of guidelines. Staff members can facilitate the transition to this new environment by spending some time researching the new setting. First, the coordinator should try to meet all relevant personnel. If transition services are to be provided at a college, this would include the staff from the college Support Services Disability Office; the faculty of relevant departments; and the heads of the facilities students may use, such as the bookstore, library, or cafeteria. If transition services are to be provided in a business or community setting, relevant personnel would include the company or business manager, supervisory staff members, and coworkers.

The hierarchy and protocol of the new setting must be understood so that the appropriate people are involved in the implementation process. Becoming familiar with the personnel also allows the coordinator to begin to identify individuals who may become potential natural supports for participating students. Researching the setting may also help to indicate other services and resources that students could use.

The coordinator may also want to familiarize him- or herself with the language of the new setting. If the site is a college, he or she should obtain a copy of the college catalog and schedule of classes. These contain important information about admissions, tuition, and the types of available courses. Finally, the coordinator should locate the college or company policies on attendance and behavior so that he or she will know the expectations personnel in that setting have for students. The more familiar staff members are with the operations and key players in the new setting, the more they will be able to facilitate a successful transition for the incoming students.

Identify Inclusive Opportunities

One purpose of providing students with significant disabilities with experiences in college or community settings is to give them opportunities to interact with people of similar ages and interests in integrated settings. Part of the planning

The following activities will assist in identifying inclusive opportunities for students:

1. Obtain a list of all college or community activities via monthly bulletin, community newspapers, or e-mail listservs.

2. Meet with the director of student activities to discuss potential connections.

3. Investigate volunteer organizations, such as Habitat for Humanity, Meals on Wheels, local animal shelters, or other volunteer organizations.

4. Investigate various religious or ethnic organizations on campus or in the community.

5. Obtain a list of all student clubs and organizations on campus.

6. Contact the presidents of fraternities and sororities to solicit their involvement.

7. Obtain a copy of the college schedule of classes, including continuing education course offerings.

8. Review course offerings and schedules to determine courses in which students might be interested.

9. Contact the Office of Disability Support Services to obtain information about course instructors, course expectations, and accommodations.

10. Contact athletics director and coaches regarding possible student involvement with campus sports or recreation activities.

Figure 2.4. Activities to identify inclusive opportunities.

PROFILE 2.2
EXAMPLE OF A SUCCESSFUL INCLUSIVE EXPERIENCE ON A COLLEGE CAMPUS

Manny had spent 5 years in a self-contained classroom in a comprehensive high school before coming to the Community Connections Program (CCP) at his local community college. He had also participated only in unpaid job-training experiences. On entering CCP, he was able to find two paid positions in the community. The best part of Manny's story, however, has to do with his love of basketball, which is Manny's favorite pastime. Whether playing or watching, Manny is all about basketball. CCP is located at a community college where Manny has the same access to the athletic facility and the basketball courts as all other college students. As he visited the courts regularly, he developed a relationship with the head basketball coach of the community college. Through this relationship, he has parlayed his love of basketball into a position on the team. Manny became one of the varsity basketball team managers. In this position, he helps with inventory, equipment, and game preparations, and he offers water and towels to the players during the games. The other members of the team have accepted Manny as one of their own. Manny often "hangs out" with the basketball team members and their friends while on campus (e.g., in the cafeteria, in the lounge).

for daily operations thus should entail becoming familiar with various places where students can meet and interact with individuals without disabilities. Time should be spent investigating college and community sites that offer work, recreational, and educational experiences involving these individuals. Figure 2.4 lists various activities that could help to identify inclusive opportunities for students. As illustrated in Profile 2.2, inclusive experiences may lead to friendships.

Determine Educational Environments and Staffing

Although services may be based in one college or community setting, students should not receive services only in that place. They should be encouraged to participate in a variety of educational environments that meet their individual needs and interests. For example, some students may be interested in participating in an activity at the community recreation center or attending a function at the public library. Staff members will need to determine how students will do these things and who will be available to provide support, if needed.

Creating a general list of the types of settings students might want to access may be helpful in determining who will be responsible for providing instruction or supervision in each setting. Obviously, the coordinator will not be able to provide instruction to students in a variety of locations at the same time, so a list of the possible support staff for each setting should also be made. All support personnel need not be from the local school system. Whenever possible, the coordinator should try to obtain instructional support from an individual who is typically a part of the environment or a natural support. Form 16: Educational Environments and Staff (see p. 76) provides a structure for identifying (a) how different environments may be used for instruction and (b) the various individuals who could supervise or teach. When students' schedules are established, this form can be used to help brainstorm about various potential support persons. Figure 2.5 is an example of a list developed using Form 16.

Determine Student Goals

After reviewing the information provided by the student and his or her family in the personal statement section of the student application (see Form 12, p. 65), the coordinator should meet individually with each student and his or her family to determine the student's personal goals. During this meeting, these individuals will review the student's previous experiences, needs, interests, and preferences and create a schedule based on this information. This is also a good time to discuss how the college or community environment may differ from high school. The coordinator also might want to provide examples of instructional activities and experiences that are possible in the new setting. In addition, having students and their families visit these settings and observe various activities may help them in conceptualizing new goals.

During this meeting, the coordinator can discuss different avenues related to employment, independent living, and social and recreational activities. For example, if a student is interested in working with animals, the coordinator might suggest obtaining work experience at a veterinarian's office or pet store, volunteering to walk dogs at the local animal shelter, or taking a course in animal grooming at the

Form 16: Educational Environments and Staff

Environment	Staff
College class/college library	Instructional assistant Best buddy College student Speech therapist Librarian Occupational therapist
Computer lab/career center	College instructor Peer Instructional assistant Career specialist Job or educational coach Coordinator
Employment setting/staff break room	Employer Coworker Job or educational coach Coordinator Rehabilitation personnel
Cafeteria/student union/bookstore	Peer Instructional assistant Best buddy College student Speech or occupational therapist
Apartment/group homes	Instructional assistant Resident Coordinator Best buddy Community adult agency personnel
Fraternities/sororities/clubs/volunteer organizations	Best buddies Classmates Student volunteer
Public transportation/college transportation	Transition teacher Work experience coordinator Coordinator Community adult agency personnel
College or community recreation program, or YMCA	Facility personnel Physical therapist Instructional assistant Student volunteer
Mall or shopping center	Speech or occupational therapist Instructional assistant Best buddy Coordinator

Figure 2.5. Example of a completed Form 16.

PROFILE 2.3.a
STUDENT IEP PARTICIPATION GOAL

Student Name: Kelly Martin   **School Year:** 2005–2006

Student Goal 1: To participate in IEP meeting and monitor progress toward goals

Upon entry: Kelly had attended IEP meetings but had never spoken during them. She had never seen or read her IEP or monitored progress toward a goal.

October: Kelly has reviewed her IEP with the coordinator and can describe the purpose of the IEP. She has created a checklist to monitor progress toward goals and reviews this checklist weekly.

December: Kelly has role-played participating in IEP meetings, including introducing herself and providing a summary of her current progress toward goals.

February: Kelly has created a PowerPoint presentation listing her current levels of performance, accomplished goals, future goals, and required supports.

May: Kelly participated in her IEP meeting, gave her PowerPoint presentation, and assisted in creating new goals for the following year.

Outcome: Kelly successfully achieved this goal and plans to continue monitoring her own progress next year through use of the checklist. Kelly also intends to invite some new people to her next IEP meeting and has helped to develop some new goals for next year.

local community college. Once a student's personal goals have been established, the coordinator will be able to identify the instructional environments best suited to those goals and to clarify the types of supports required to achieve each goal.

Form 17: Student Goals (see p. 77) may be used to document each goal; it provides space for the student and coordinator to monitor progress toward the goals on a quarterly basis. Examples of student goals for participation in the IEP process, transportation, and employment are provided in Profiles 2.3.a, 2.3.b, and 2.3.c. These profiles demonstrate how Form 17 can be used to document and monitor goals in any area. These forms should be completed in collaboration with the student, and copies can be kept in the student's file or portfolio. Students could also use these forms to facilitate discussion of their progress toward IEP goals and objectives during annual IEP meetings.

Purchase or Develop Curricula

After the goals have been determined, the coordinator should decide if new instructional materials or curricula need to be purchased or developed. Materials

PROFILE 2.3.b
STUDENT TRAVEL TRAINING GOAL

Student Name: Marcus Machelli   **School Year:** 2005–2006

Student Goal 1: To travel independently on a public bus to and from his worksite, his college, and his home.

Upon entry: Marcus had ridden public transportation on community outings as part of a group but had never negotiated public transportation without supervision.

October: Marcus reviewed bus schedules and can now discern which bus he needs to take to go from college to work and back. He participates in travel training once weekly with a job coach.

December: Marcus has ridden public transportation to work from the college with minimal supervision (job coach followed in car). He continues to get rides from his parent to go to work from home.

February: Marcus has begun to take the bus to work from his home with supervision. (Three transfers are required.) Marcus is independently navigating the bus system to work from the college.

May: Marcus rides the bus independently to and from work from both the college and home. Marcus has begun to access other bus routes to get to the mall and to participate in other community resources and social activities.

Outcome: Marcus successfully achieved his goal and plans to expand his use of the public transportation system by using it to visit relatives in other parts of the county.

related to writing résumés, developing word processing skills, navigating the Internet, handling banking, developing self-determination skills, and using public transportation may be appropriate. The coordinator and the committee should work together to determine the budget for purchasing materials and should set aside some planning time to familiarize themselves with what may need to be purchased or developed.

Develop Weekly Schedules and Individual Student Schedules

After gathering information on the new setting, the potential learning environments, and the students' personal goals, the coordinator should create a weekly schedule using Form 18: Master Schedule (see p. 78). This schedule, as illustrated in Figure 2.6, will be an overview of the student's activities, the instructional settings, and the support staff in each setting. When creating this schedule, the coordinator should consider whether students will be required to participate in activities every day. Due to the flexible nature of college and community settings, it

**PROFILE 2.3.c
STUDENT EMPLOYMENT GOAL**

Student Name: Dwayne Rodgers   **School Year:** 2005–2006

Student Goal 1: To obtain paid employment in an office setting

Upon entry: Dwayne had worked in a fast-food establishment, making $5.15 an hour, and had previous unpaid work experience in the public library.

October: Dwayne took an interest inventory. Dwayne and his coordinator reviewed the results of the inventory and talked about Dwayne's preferred job characteristics and goals. Dwayne wants to learn how to be a receptionist in an office setting.

December: Dwayne visited three office settings (medical, dental, business) to job shadow a receptionist. Dwayne enjoyed the business office setting the most and determined that support would be needed in typing and filing.

February: Dwayne interviewed for two jobs and was hired by Malcolm Industries as a part-time receptionist, making $5.15 an hour. He works 3 days a week for 4 hours a day. He received on-the-job training and support from the job coach daily.

May: Dwayne continues his schedule at Malcolm Industries and plans to increase his hours over the summer. His job coach now checks in twice a month, and Dwayne has received his first evaluation and a small pay raise (to $5.35 an hour).

Outcome: Dwayne successfully achieved his goal and hopes to maintain this job through his remaining school year. He has expressed interest in expanding his job duties to include filing microfiche and learning data entry.

may be possible for students to work on some days and receive transition services at the college or community site on other days. Planning time for networking with college instructors, developing jobs, planning lessons, and meeting with community agency personnel should also be built in by the coordinator, because these activities are crucial to the development of inclusive student opportunities. A copy of the weekly schedule should be posted so that it is accessible to both staff and students.

As students' schedules become more varied, Form 18 may be used to create individual student schedules, which should provide an overview of each student's weekly schedule and may be easier for the students to use independently. Each student should have a copy of his or her own schedule, as demonstrated in Profile 2.4.

Monitor Staff and Student Activities

Once transition services have been implemented and student and staff schedules are in place, student and staff activities should be monitored on a regular basis.

Form 18: Master Schedule

Time	Monday	Tuesday	Wednesday	Thursday	Friday
7:00 a.m.					Work 8–3 (S, K)
8:00 a.m.	Travel training (F, K, w/IA1) Arrive at college (C, S, B, M) Work 8–1 (J)	Travel training (C, M, w/IA2) Work 8–3 (J)	Travel training (F, K, w/IA) Arrive at college Work 8–1 (J)	Travel training (C, B, w/IA2) Work 8–1 (J)	Recreation Center (J, C, B, w/IA1 & NS) Independent work on college campus (M, F, w/IA2 & CO)
9:00 a.m.	Review schedule/ independent work/ self-determination (B, C, S, M, w/IA2 & CO)	Work Super Plaza (IA1) PETsMART (B) Borders (C) Home Depot (K)	Review schedule/ independent work/ self-determination (B, C, S, M, w/IA2 & CO)	Work Super Plaza (CO & IA1) PETsMART (B) Borders (C) Home Depot (K)	Independent work/ self-determination/ on college campus (J, C, B, w/ST & CO) Student union/college Activity (M, F, w/IA1 & IA2)
10:00 a.m.	College classes Tai Chi (F, C, w/IA) Navigating the Internet (S, M, w/IA2) Planning time (CO) Aerobics (B, K, w/NS & PT)	Cherry Hill Mall (CO & IA2) Radio Shack (M) Popeyes (S) Sears (F)	College classes Tai Chi (F, C, w/IA) Navigating the Internet (S, M, w/IA) Planning time (CO) Aerobics (B, K, w/NS & PT)	Cherry Hill Mall (IA2) Radio Shack (M) Popeyes (S) Sears (F)	
11:00 a.m.					Lunch 11:30 (B, F)
12:00 p.m.	Lunch in cafeteria (B, K, S, C) Work 12–4 (M, F)	Lunch in community (B, C, K, w/IA2) Lunch on campus (M, S, F, w/BB)	Lunch in cafeteria (B, K, S, C) Work 12–4 (M, F)	Lunch in community (B, C, K, w/IA) Lunch on campus (M, S, F, J, w/IA2)	Lunch in cafeteria (J, C, M) Work 12–4 (B, F)
1:00 p.m.	College computer lab (S, B, K, w/IA) College library (C w/NS) College class—Poetry (J w/CO)		College computer lab (S, B, K, w/IA) College library (CL/NS) College class—Poetry (J w/CO)		Community Metro access and travel training 1–2:45 (J, C, M, w/IA2 & CO)
2:00 p.m.	Work 2–3:30 (S w/IA2) Bus home (B, K, C)	Library/résumé (K, S, w/CO) Independent work on campus (B, C w/IA) Community recreation center (M, F, w/NS)	Work 2–3:30 (S w/IA2) Bus home (B, K, C, J)	Library/résumé (K, J, S, w/CO) Independent work on campus (B, C, w/IA) Community recreation center (M, F, w/NS)	
3:00 p.m.					

Note. This format can be used for both the weekly schedule and the student schedule.

Figure 2.6. Example of a completed Form 18.

KEY

Students

J = Joe
S = Sue
B = Bernardo
F = Frieda
K = Kayla
C = Colin
M = Margaret

Staff

CO = Coordinator
IA1 & IA2 = instructional assistants
PT = physical therapist
ST = speech therapist

Support Persons

BB = best buddy
NS = natural support

PROFILE 2.4
BOB'S SCHEDULE

Time	Monday	Tuesday	Wednesday	Thursday	Friday
7:00 a.m.	Bob rides city bus to college campus				
8:00 a.m.	Functional instruction with coordinator in classroom on college campus	Career planning or self-determination skills instruction with coordinator	Free time—Bob gets to campus in time for weight-training class	Career planning or self-determination skills instruction with coordinator	Functional instruction with coordinator in classroom on college campus
9:00 a.m.		Ceramics class—in art building with natural supports		Ceramics class—in art building with natural supports	Independent study and tutoring from special education intern at library
9:30 a.m.	Weight-training class at fitness center		Weight-training class at fitness center		
10:00 a.m.					
10:30 a.m.		Travel training/community skills training with teaching assistant and two other students		Travel training/community skills training with teaching assistant and two other students	
11:00 a.m.	College computer lab with special education intern (peer tutor)		College computer lab with special education intern (peer tutor)		Lunch and social activity with fraternity brothers on campus

Review schedule w/coordinator |
12:00 p.m.	Lunch with other students or best buddy at student union food court	Lunch in community with peers	Lunch with peer tutor at student union food court	Lunch in community with peers	
1:00 p.m.	Go to city bus stop on campus—go to job site	Audit college class: Navigating the Internet, with coordinator	Go to city bus stop on campus—go to job site	Audit college class: Navigating the Internet, with coordinator	Go to city bus stop on campus—go to job site
2:00 p.m.	Work part time at pet store		Work part time at pet store		Work part time at pet store
3:00 p.m.		School bus picks Bob up on campus		School bus picks Bob up on campus	
4:00 p.m.					
5:00 p.m.	Parents pick Bob up from work		Parents pick Bob up from work		A friend picks Bob up from work

(continues)

Doing so will allow the coordinator to track student participation in employment, college courses, and community and campus activities. Staff time and responsibilities can also be documented. This information can be compiled at the end of the year and presented to the committee or school board. (Directions for compiling monitoring data will be presented in Chapter 3.)

PROFILE 2.4
Continued.

As shown on his schedule, Bob is participating in a variety of activities, including two college courses, a weight-training class, and a job at a pet store. One of the college courses he attends is a ceramic arts class. He is taking this class for credit, and in it he receives natural support from his peers and the college instructor. Bob is auditing his other course, Navigating the Internet; in this course, he receives support from his coordinator. Through the Peer Tutoring Office, he developed a relationship with a student who belongs to a fraternity on campus. Bob goes out for lunch or "hangs out" with his friends at the fraternity house on Friday afternoons. If he doesn't have to work, sometimes he will spend the afternoon shooting pool with guys in the student union.

Bob works on his college courses, résumé building, or interviewing skills four mornings a week, for an hour, with his coordinator. He also spends some of this time working on his self-determination skills and is hoping to run his next IEP meeting and conduct a PowerPoint presentation highlighting his accomplishments this year. Bob works a few times a week in the computer lab or library with college students from the Peer Tutoring Office at the college. Bob knows how to ride the local bus to the college and to his job site, but he still is not comfortable with the bus route back to his house, which is a bit more complicated. The instructional assistant is working twice a week on travel training with Bob and two other students to address this need. Bob's job at the pet store initially was a training position, but Bob excelled at his restocking job and now works for a dollar more than minimum wage. He has begun to assist in the puppy training classes and hopes to expand his hours to work on the weekends.

Monitoring Student Activities

Student activities may be monitored by completing three simple data forms that track students' employment experiences, college class participation, and recreational activity participation. Form 19: Student Employment (see p. 79) may be used to monitor job experiences. As illustrated in Figure 2.7, this form details the number of jobs a student has secured during a school year, the duration of each job, whether the job was on campus or off campus, the pay rate, the hours worked, the types of benefits received (if any), the level of support required, and the reason the job ended.

Form 20: College or Adult Education Courses (see p. 80) may be used to monitor course enrollment. This form documents the courses each student has taken, the instructor for each course, whether the course was for credit or audit, the tuition cost, the course schedule, and the level of educational support provided. Figure 2.8 is an example of a completed form. In this example, the tuition for the courses taken by students was waived because the students were recipients of Supplemental Security Income, or SSI. Many community colleges have a policy of waiving tuition for students who receive SSI.

Finally, the kinds of extracurricular activities in which students are participating may be documented in Form 21: College and Community Activities (see p. 81). This form contains space to list the college or community social, athletic, fine or performing arts, or other extracurricular activities in which students might engage

(text continues on p. 60)

Form 19: Student Employment
2005–2006 School Year

Student Name	Job	Start Date	Location (CC or CM)	Paid or Unpaid	$/Hr	Benefits	Hrs/Wk	Support Person/ Support Code	End Date/Reason for Leaving
John	Dishwasher/Out-back Steakhouse	9/27/05	CM	Paid	5.15	None	10	Job coach/WC	12/15/05 Laid off
	Busboy/Pizza Hut	1/15/06	CM	Paid	5.25	None	15	VR/MC	4/15/06 Promoted
	Host/Pizza Hut	4/15/06	CM	Paid	5.35	None	20	VR/MC	
Juanita	Vet asst./ PETsMART	10/31/05	CM	Paid	5.25	None	12	Job coach/WC	
Chelsea	Receptionist/ Student Union	2/25/06	CC	Paid	5.35	None	10	Job coach/MC	
Leroy	Laborer/ACME Construction	11/20/05	CM	Unpaid	N/A	None	10	Job coach/WT	
Shawn	Tech asst./ Jiffy Lube	10/16/05	CM	Unpaid	N/A	None	12	Job coach/WC	

Note. Location codes: CC = college campus; CM = community. Support Codes: DT = daily training; WT = weekly training; WC = weekly check-in; MC = monthly check-in; VR = vocational rehabilitation.

Figure 2.7. Example of a completed Form 19.

57

Form 20: College or Adult Education Courses
2005–2006 School Year

Student Name	Course(s) Taken	Semester	Instructor	Credits/ Certification(s) Earned	Audit	Tuition & Fees	Class Schedule	Support
John	Weight Training	Fall '05	Tyler	3	No	Waived/$28	M/W 10–11:15	M
	Keyboarding	Spring '06	Carlton	0	Yes	Waived/$28	M/W 1–2:15	D
Juanita	Intro to Pet Care	Fall '05	Simpson	0	Yes	Waived/$28	T/TH 9–10:30	C
Chelsea	Keyboarding	Spring '06	Carlton	0	Yes	Waived/$28	M/W 1–2:15	D
Leroy	Weight Training	Fall '05	Tyler	3	No	Waived/$28	M/W 10–11:15	M
Shawn	Tai Chi	Spring '06	Kim	3	No	Waived/$28	M/W/F 8–9	M

Note. Support codes: D = daily (daily accompany student to class and provide assistance with assignments); M = monitor (check with student and instructor biweekly, modify assignments and tests); C = check-in (check with instructor at the beginning of the semester and periodically throughout the course).

Figure 2.8. Example of a completed Form 20.

Form 21: College and Community Activities
20<u>05</u>–20<u>06</u> School Year

List all college or community social, athletic, fine or performing arts, or other extra-curricular activities that students attend on a regular basis.

Student Name	Activity	Location (College or Community)	How Often	Educational Support
John	Photography Club	College	2x/month	C
Juanita	Aerobics	Community: YMCA	2x/week	M
Chelsea	Delta Pi Sorority	College	1x/week	M
Leroy	African American Student Union	College	2x/month	M
Shawn	Student Advocacy Group	College	2x/month	C

Note. Support Codes: D = daily (daily accompany student to activity and provide support); M = monitor (monitor student on a weekly basis); C = check-in (check in with student periodically).

Figure 2.9. Example of a completed Form 21.

on a regular basis. This form allows for documenting activities both at the college and in the community, the frequency of student participation, and the level of support required. An example of a completed form is provided in Figure 2.9.

Monitoring Staff Activities

How staff members spend their time should also be monitored. Information to be collected includes the number of hours per week spent on providing job development, job support, travel training, college classroom support, or community-based instruction. Coordinators may want to document the amount of time they spend meeting with college and community personnel to obtain new opportunities for the students being served.

The purposes of monitoring staff time are to determine which activities require the greatest staff support and to identify areas on which staff may need to spend more time, such as employment support or educational coaching. This information may be compiled on Form 22: Staff Activities and Time Allocation (see p. 82). Each staff member should complete a form, providing an estimate of the number of hours spent on each activity for each day. Figure 2.10 is an example of a form completed by a paraprofessional documenting the amount of time spent on each activity during a week in October. These kinds of data do not have to be collected daily, but they should be noted at regular intervals (e.g., monthly, quarterly).

Form 22: Staff Activities and Time Allocation

Staff Name: Sally T.

Staff Position: Paraprofessional

Week of: 10/22/05

Total Hours Worked: 35

Activity	Monday	Tuesday	Wednesday	Thursday	Friday	Total Hours	%
In-Class Support	1	.5	.75	0	1.25	3.5	10
College Class Support	.75	.25	.75	1	.75	3.5	10
Employment Support	2	1	2.5	1.5	3.5	10.5	30
Accessing Community	.25	2	1	2	0	5.25	15
Transportation	.75	.75	.75	.75	.5	3.5	10
Networking	0	1.25	0	.5	0	1.75	5
Data Collection	1.25	1	1	1	1	5.25	15
Administrative Duties	1	.25	.25	.25	0	1.75	5
Other							
Other							
Other							
Other							
Total Hours	7	7	7	7	7	35	100

Figure 2.10. Example of a completed Form 22.

APPENDIX

Chapter 2
Reproducible Forms

Form 11: Overview

Description:

Staffing:

Liability:

Facilities:

Collaborators:

Transportation:

Outcomes:

Timeline:

Evaluation:

Form 12: Student Application

This application should be completed by the referring teacher, the student, and his or her family. All questions must be answered completely for the application to be accepted. Once completed, please return this application to _____

by _____.   (*fill in name*)

      (*fill in date*)

Personal Information

(*to be compiled by the student and family*)

Name: Date of Birth:

Age: Social Security Number:

Address:

E-Mail Address:

Name of Parent or Guardian:

Home Phone: Mother's Work Phone: Father's Work Phone:

                Mother's E-Mail Address: Father's E-Mail Address:

Home School: Home School Phone/Extension:

Referring Teacher:

Is Receiving Services From:
- ☐ Supplemental Security Income   ☐ Social Security Disability Insurance
- ☐ Developmental Disabilities Administration
- ☐ Medical Assistance   ☐ Vocational Rehabilitation

School Information

(*to be completed by referring teacher*)

List the names of schools and years of attendance.

Names of Schools   **Years of Attendance**

_____

_____

_____

_____

Anticipated Exit Date:

(continues)

Form 12: Student Application *Continued.*

Personal Statement

(This portion of the application should be completed with the student.)

Why do you want to receive services in a college setting?

_____

_____

What do you want to learn that you have not been able to learn in high school?

_____

_____

What kinds of jobs are you interested in after you leave school?

_____

_____

What do you do in your free time?

_____

_____

What is your favorite hobby or sport?

_____

What is your favorite musical group or who is your favorite singer?

_____

Do you spend time with friends outside of school?   Yes   No
If yes, what do you like to do with your friends?

_____

What types of things do you need assistance with?

_____

(continues)

Below, please describe some of the skills you would like to learn.

Continuing education (e.g., community college classes)

_____

Independent living (e.g., cooking, housekeeping)

_____

Functional academics (e.g., reading, calculating, budgeting)

_____

Social/recreational/leisure (e.g., making friends, going places)

_____

Vocational training (e.g., applications, job experiences, interview skills)

_____

Work Information
(to be completed by transition or work coordinator)

Has the student demonstrated success in at least four semesters of supported or independent work experience (unpaid job tryouts) in the community or the school?

Yes   No

If yes, please list work experiences and level of support required. (Does the student require one-to-one supervision or periodic support to perform the job, or does she or he work independently?)

Job Description	Dates of Experience	Level of Support	Reason for Leaving

If no, why has the student not participated in four semesters of work experience?

_____

_____

_____

(continues)

Form 12: Student Application *Continued.*

Has the student held a paid job in the community?   Yes   No

If yes, please list the jobs held, the dates of employment, the level of support, wages received, and the student's reason for leaving.

Job Description	Dates of Employment	Level of Support	Wages Per Hour	Reason for Leaving

Is the student currently employed in his or her neighborhood?   Yes   No

Does the student require specialized equipment, adaptations or modifications, or specific reinforcers at the workplace? If so, please describe:

_____

If the student has not been engaged in a paid employment position, why not?

_____

Inclusion Information
(to be completed by referring teacher)

Has the student participated in general education classes in his or her home school this year?
Yes   No

If yes, please list the subjects and teachers:

Subject(s)   **Teacher(s)**

_____

_____

_____

_____

What accommodations were used to support the student in these classes?

_____

_____

_____

(continues)

Identify learning strategies used to facilitate a positive experience.

_____

_____

_____

Behavior Information
(to be completed by referring teacher)

Does the student demonstrate satisfactory school attendance as defined by the board of education?　　Yes　　　No

If no, please explain:

_____

_____

Does the student demonstrate satisfactory school behavior?　　Yes　　　No

If no, please describe the nature of the student's behavioral misconduct and attach incident reports:

_____

_____

Has the student ever been suspended or expelled?　　Yes　　　No

If yes, what was the nature of the offense?

_____

_____

How was the suspension or expulsion resolved?

_____

_____

(continues)

Form 12: Student Application *Continued.*

How would this student handle the following scenarios?

A professor is absent and has left a note on the door stating that class has been canceled.

_____

_____

_____

During class, the fire alarm goes off and the building is being evacuated.

_____

_____

_____

An unknown adult asks the student to come with him or her.

_____

_____

_____

Note. Modified and reprinted with the permission of D. Fischer, Anne Arundel County Public School System, Maryland.

Form 13: Transportation Plan Checklist

Please review with your committee the following questions related to transportation.

- Will the local school system provide transportation?
- What times will transportation be available?
- Will parents need to provide any transportation?
- Will students need to travel independently?
- Is specialized transportation (e.g., a wheelchair lift) needed?
- Who will provide travel training?
- When will travel training occur?
- Will transportation be available for community-based instruction?
- Will transportation be available for travel to and from employment?
- Must students going to paid jobs provide their own transportation?
- Can staff members transport students in their own vehicles?
- Will students go directly from home to the postsecondary site, or will they need to be dropped off at a high school and then take another bus to the post-secondary site?

Other transportation-related issues:

This page intentionally left blank.

Form 14: Written Agreement

Between _____ and _____

(school or school system)

This AGREEMENT, made on _____ by and between the _____

(date)   *(name of school or school system)*

Board of Education _____ and the _____

(address)   *(name of institution or organization)*

_____, hereby follows:

(address)

---

1. Scope of Services

2. Duties of the BCPS Board

3. Duties of the Institution

(continues)

4. **Fees**

5. **Liability Insurance and Indemnification**

6. **Term and Termination**

Signatures and Titles

_____   _____

_____   _____

_____   _____

Form 15: Policy Checklist

Graduation Policy
- After 4 years, will students participate in a high school graduation ceremony prior to receiving services at the college or community site?
- Will students receiving services at the postsecondary site receive a mock certificate (not their real certificate) at the high school graduation ceremony?
- Will students receiving services at the college or community site have a graduation ceremony when they leave the school system?

Record-Keeping and Finance Policy
- What school will the program or services be directly connected to for record keeping (attendance, files)?
- Will the designated school count the students in its full-time equivalent enrollment (FTE)?
- If no, who gets the dollars that follow the students?
- How will the coordinator access the budget?

Administrative Policy
- Who will be the principal or administrator in charge of the program or services?
- Where will IEP meetings be held?
- Who will case-manage the IEPs?
- How will related services, such as speech and language therapy, physical or occupational therapy, or psychological services or counseling, be provided?
- What meetings (e.g., faculty meetings at high school), if any, must the coordinator attend?
- To whom will the coordinator report?

Permission and Waiver Policy
- How will students receive medication, if needed?
- Where will medication be housed?
- Is a medical waiver needed?
- Is a transportation waiver needed?
- Is a publicity waiver (for pictures or videotaping) needed?

Free and Reduced Lunch Policy
- How will recipients of free and reduced lunch be served?
(For example, students could use ID cards to purchase lunch and bill the local school system, or the lunches could be picked up from a nearby school building daily.)

Emergency Procedures
- What is the procedure to be followed in case of a medical emergency (illness or injury)?
- What is the procedure to be followed in case of disruptive or dangerous behavior?
- What is the procedure to be followed in case of student flight?

Scheduling Policy
- What will be the policy for inclement weather?
- How will services be provided at the college or community site during semester breaks, spring breaks, and holidays?

Form 16: Educational Environments and Staff

Environment	Staff

Form 17: Student Goals

Student Name:	School Year:

Student Goal

Upon Entry:

October:

December:

February:

May:

Outcome:

Form 18: Master Schedule

Time	Monday	Tuesday	Wednesday	Thursday	Friday
7:00 a.m.					
8:00 a.m.					
9:00 a.m.					
10:00 a.m.					
11:00 a.m.					
12:00 p.m.					
1:00 p.m.					
2:00 p.m.					
3:00 p.m.					

Note. This format can be used for both the weekly schedule and the student schedule.

Form 19: Student Employment
20___–20___ School Year

Student Name	Job	Start Date	Location (CC or CM)	Paid or Unpaid	$/Hr	Benefits	Hrs/Wk	Support Person/ Support Code	End Date/Reason for Leaving

Note. Location codes: CC = college campus; CM = community. Support Codes: DT = daily training; WT = weekly training; WC = weekly check-in; MC = monthly check-in; VR = vocational rehabilitation.

Form 20: College or Adult Education Courses

20__–20__ School Year

Student Name	Course(s) Taken	Semester	Instructor	Credits/ Certification(s) Earned	Audit	Tuition & Fees	Class Schedule	Support

Note. Support codes: D = daily (daily accompany student to class and provide assistance with assignments); M = monitor (check with student and instructor biweekly, modify assignments and tests); C = check-in (check with instructor at the beginning of the semester and periodically throughout the course).

Form 21: College and Community Activities
20__–20__ School Year

List all college or community social, athletic, fine or performing arts, or other extra-curricular activities that students attend on a regular basis.

Student Name	Activity	Location (College or Community)	How Often	Educational Support

Note. Support Codes: D = daily (daily accompany student to activity and provide support);
M = monitor (monitor student on a weekly basis); C = check-in (check in with student periodically).

Form 22: Staff Activities and Time Allocation

Staff Name: _____   Staff Position: _____

Week of: _____   Total Hours Worked: _____

Activity	Monday	Tuesday	Wednesday	Thursday	Friday	Total Hours	%
In-Class Support							
College Class Support							
Employment Support							
Accessing Community							
Transportation							
Networking							
Data Collection							
Administrative Duties							
Other							
Other							
Other							
Other							
Total Hours							

CHAPTER 3
Evaluation

Evaluation activities must be included in the overall design of transition services in college and community settings. These components of the program will help in determining if the service-delivery goals have been met and when they need to be revised or expanded. Evaluation processes will also help document the types of activities in which students have participated, along with satisfaction with services and supports on the part of students, families, teachers, and community personnel. One of these activities should be follow-up of students after they exit the school system to determine postsecondary outcomes. Once compiled, evaluation data can be used to convince advisory and school boards that transition services in college or community settings promote integrated community experiences and optimal outcomes.

An evaluation plan should include methods for collecting information on staff and students' activities on an ongoing basis. This will save time in the long run and provide important information to the advisory committee, school system personnel, and consumers and families. In education, we often "know" an approach works; however, it is important to document why a particular approach works and to be able to advocate for the expansion of such efforts based on reliable and valid information. Including evaluation methods in the planning and implementation stages will help the planners determine if the new transition services are effective in achieving both desired student goals and outcomes and participant satisfaction. In addition, planners will be able to see if these services are being implemented as had been envisioned and if changes are needed to improve student experiences and outcomes.

DESIGNING THE EVALUATION

Just as each setting will be unique in terms of location, students served, and supports provided, each evaluation design will also be different. We suggest designing evaluation activities in terms of the following:

1. compiling monitoring data on student and staff activities,
2. documenting student outcomes, and
3. assessing participant satisfaction.

Each of these activities is explained in this chapter, and sample forms are provided. This discussion is followed by a review of how to (a) determine a schedule for evaluation activities; (b) assign personnel to collect and compile the information and data; and (c) review and share evaluation data with the advisory committee, school board, or other pertinent parties.

Compiling Data

In Chapter 2 we described how to collect data to monitor student employment experiences, course enrollment, and participation in college and community activities. We also discussed how to monitor staff activities and time usage. This information may be compiled to provide a summary of staff and student activities throughout the year. This summary will allow the coordinator and advisory committee to determine if transition services are meeting student goals and if changes need to be made to daily operations or staffing.

Student Activities and Achievements

To compile monitoring information on student activities, Form 23: Compilation of Student Activities (see p. 94) may be used. This form can be completed once or twice a year to provide a summary of students' activities, as illustrated in Figure 3.1. All of the information needed to complete this form is available on the student activities forms—19, 20, and 21—provided in Chapter 2 (see pp. 79–81). Once compiled, this information may be used to provide an update of student activities to the advisory committee, school board personnel, and parents and to ascertain the extent to which these activities reflect the chosen goals.

Form 24: Compilation of Student Goal Achievement (see p. 95) contains spaces for listing the number of goals that were met, the number of goals that were not met, the reason these goals were not met, and the response. Student goals initially were documented on Form 17 in Chapter 2 (see p. 77), along with anecdotal notes on progress. Completing Form 24 requires reviewing each student's file and determining the number of goals that were and were not achieved. If the majority of student goals were successfully met, this form will indicate the positive effect the provided services have had on student achievement. A large number of unmet goals should be a red flag. These goals should be carefully reviewed to determine why they were not met and if changes are needed to the goals or to student supports. Figure 3.2 provides a sample completed Form 24.

Staff Activities

As noted previously, staff members' time and responsibilities should be monitored using Form 22, found in Chapter 2 (see p. 82). Compiling this information will indicate the percentage of time staff members spend on the major activities. This can be accomplished by using Form 25: Compilation of Staff Activities (see p. 96). Once staff time usage has been determined, recommendations may be made regarding reallocating staff time from one activity to another, as illustrated in Profile 3.1. Another use of these data might be to advocate for additional staff positions. Figure 3.3 demonstrates how Form 25 can be completed.

Student Outcomes After Exiting School

As a student is ready to exit the school system, the coordinator should create a file for him or her that documents his or her status upon exit. Things to be considered include the student's job, rate of pay, benefits received, adult services provided, current eligibility for services (SSI, SSDI), and the number and kind of activities in which the student participates weekly (classes, community events, recreational activities). Form 26: Student Exit Information (see p. 97) provides space for recording each of these areas.

Form 23: Compilation of Student Activities
20<u>05</u>–20<u>06</u> School Year

Date: **5/21/06**

Name and Title of Person Completing Form: **Sandra M., Coordinator**

Student Activities

Fill in the blank for each of the following questions:

10 Total number of students served
3 Number of students who attended college/adult education courses for credit
5 Number of students who attended college/adult education courses for audit
2 Number of students participating in college courses informally
2 Number of students receiving certification
5 Number of students regularly (≥ 2x/mo) participating in clubs and organizations on campus

3 Number of students regularly participating (≥ 2x/mo) in recreational activities in the community
1 Number of students working full time
$5.75 Average rate of pay (FT)
7 Number of students working part time
$5.40 Average rate of pay (PT)
2 Number of students in unpaid training sites
3.5 Average hours of job support from staff
1 Number of students receiving services from agencies serving adults

---

List college courses taken: **Aerobics, Keyboarding, Art, Basic Math**

Other:

List paid job locations: **Wendy's, Wal-Mart, Bernthal Micromedia, Sunrise House, PETsMART, Sennia Graphics**

List clubs/organizations accessed on campus: **Best Buddies, Hebrew Alliance, Small House Theater Players**

List community recreation facilities accessed: **YMCA, Public Library, Therapeutic Riding**

Recommendations for changes/improvements: *Identify additional on-campus opportunities for students to join clubs, locate new paid training sites, obtain full-time employment for exiting students*

Recommended changes in goals: *Strengthen partnerships with service agencies to provide students with earlier access to services*

Note. Compile information from Forms 19–21 in Chapter 2 on this form.

Figure 3.1. Example of a completed Form 23.

Form 24: Compilation of Student Goal Achievement
2005–2006 School Year

Student Name	Date	# of Goals Met	# of Goals Unmet	Unmet Goals(s) and Reason	Response to Unmet Goals
Jorge	5/23/06	4	1	Independent Metro use. Student moved away from Metro stop and doesn't use it to commute to work.	Student began training on local bus route to commute to and from work and home.
Kathleen	5/26/06	4	2	Audit college art class. Classes were only offered at night. Student had no transportation.	Student took an aerobics class, T–Th, from 1–2:30.
				Obtain paid employment in animal-related field. Currently no job openings.	Student is in unpaid job placement at Giant Foods.
Fred	5/29/06	5	0		
Tanya	5/30/06	3	2	Join photography club on campus. Meeting schedule conflicted with job.	Student is exploring photography clubs off campus.
				Change job duties at restaurant. Currently no hostess opening available.	Student began to bus tables instead of hostessing.

Total number of goals met: 16

Total number of goals not met: 5

Figure 3.2. Example of a completed Form 24.

PROFILE 3.1

EXAMPLE OF CHANGES IN STAFF ACTIVITIES

Sandra M., the coordinator of services at Buckman County Community College, and her staff completed Form 22 on a quarterly basis and have compiled those data on Form 25, as shown in Figure 3.3. By reviewing the percentage of time staff members spent on various activities, they were able to determine that the majority of time was spent on employment support. More staff time is needed in the areas of college class support and transportation, however. After review of these data, Sandra held a meeting with her support staff, and they examined their students' schedules to determine how better to meet the need for staffing in college classes and transportation. On average, 15% of staff and coordinator time was devoted to providing in-class support. Sandra and the staff decided that students would be better served if their classroom instruction was reduced by 5% overall. In addition, support staff members would take on an additional half-hour of in-class support on Mondays and Wednesdays so that Sandra could provide college class support to one additional student. Sandra also decided to reduce her networking time by 10% for the remainder of the year so that she could help with travel training for students to prepare them for their summer employment. For the following year, staff members also decided that they would investigate a mentoring program in the employment sites so that more employment support would be provided via natural supports, thus freeing up staff time for other activities, such as travel training.

The coordinator should ensure that the contact information for the student and for his or her family members, employer, and service providers is current so that follow-up can be conducted. Former students should be contacted on a regular basis (we suggest every year, to start) to determine if outcomes have remained the same or changed. Phone or e-mail contact is probably the most effective way to connect with former students. Any changes may be recorded on Form 27: Follow-Up Information (see p. 98). A new sheet should be completed for each year that follow-up is conducted. Positive outcomes will encourage administrative and parental support for the services provided at the college or community site. If the outcomes are not positive, the advisory committee and program staff members should review their current practices to determine how they could be changed to better meet the students' needs.

For example, if follow-up activities show that many students were not participating in community activities after exiting school, it may be necessary to provide students with greater opportunities to build those skills while they are still in school. Once follow-up data are collected, they can be easily compiled. Student outcomes can be presented to the advisory board, school administrators, and parents using Form 28: Compilation of Follow-Up Information (see p. 99). An example of how outcome data were used to improve students' satisfaction with their post-school employment service providers is illustrated in Profile 3.2.

Form 25: Compilation of Staff Activities
20<u>05</u>–20<u>06</u> School Year

Date: 5/23/06

Name and Title of Person Completing Form: Sandra M., Coordinator

Staff Activities

Fill in the percentage of time spent on the following activities:

	In-Class Support	College Class Support	Employment Support	Community Access	Transportation (Travel Training)	Networking	Data Collection	Administrative Duties	Other
Coordinator	20%	10%	15%	10%	5%	25%	5%	10%	
Support Staff	10%	10%	30%	15%	10%	5%	15%	5%	
Average	15%	10%	22.5%	12.5%	7.5%	15%	10%	7.5%	

The majority of staff time is spent on: Employment support

More staff time is needed for the following activities: College class support and transportation

Less staff time should be spent on the following activities: In-class support

Recommendation for changes in staffing or staff activities: Support staff can increase time spent on networking duties and in-class support to provide coordinator with increased time for college class support.

Note. Compile information from Form 22 in Chapter 2 on this form.

Figure 3.3. Form 25: Sample compilation of staff activities.

Monitoring Satisfaction: Is Everybody Happy?

Another evaluation method is to determine the level of satisfaction of all the involved individuals. This would include the students, their families, college personnel, employers, community rehabilitation staff, and other agency personnel. The staff and local school personnel who are involved in referring students or supporting them in the community may also provide input.

There are a number of ways to obtain information regarding satisfaction with services. Short questionnaires, such as the surveys on Forms 29, 30, 31, and 32 (see pp. 100–103), may be used to gather input from parents, students, peers, and

PROFILE 3.2

USING OUTCOME DATA TO IMPROVE SERVICES

The Buckman County Public Schools (BCPS) staff members at Buckman County Community College conducted a telephone follow-up survey of their graduates from the previous 2 years. The outcome data they gathered indicated that the majority of the students who had graduated were not receiving services from the same service provider with whom they had been connected when they graduated. Students indicated that two of the major community providers of employment support did not provide individual competitive or supported employment placements, instead placing students in sheltered employment situations. Based on this input, the BCPS staff decided to look for additional community providers that stressed individualized placements in community employment. Staff members also summarized their findings and presented them to current students and their families to help them to make informed choices when selecting their future providers.

college staff. It sometimes may be difficult, however, to get individuals to return completed surveys. Another method is conducting short interviews on the phone or in person. For students, we suggest holding a short focus group in which they can talk about what they like, what they would change, and if they would recommend this experience to others. Students' comments about these and other issues may be considered when planning for the following year. Once this information is collected, it should be organized on Form 33: Satisfaction Data Summary (see p. 104) for the advisory committee and staff to review. Feedback should be provided to the persons who completed questionnaires to let them know how the information was used. Profile 3.3 describes how survey data were used in one situation to improve services provided in a college setting.

EVALUATION PROCESS

The evaluation process includes deciding on a schedule for evaluation activities; assigning personnel to collect and compile the information and data; and reviewing and sharing evaluation data with the advisory committee, school board, or other pertinent parties. The last step in this process would be to ascertain whether new goals, sites, services, or personnel will be needed in the next school year.

Determine a Schedule for Evaluation Activities

Once the advisory committee and program staff understand the evaluation methods that will be used, a schedule should be created using Form 34: Evaluation Activities Schedule (see p. 105). For example, monitoring activities may occur throughout the school year and be compiled at quarterly intervals. Satisfaction surveys may need to be completed only once or twice a year. Assessing student goal achievement during the school year may occur twice a year or quarterly.

PROFILE 3.3

USING SURVEY DATA TO IMPROVE SERVICES

The Buckman County Public Schools (BCPS) staff at Buckman County Community College conducted a satisfaction survey of the college faculty from whom their students were taking classes. Overall, the responses were positive, with instructors stating that they felt they understood the needs of the students with disabilities in their classes and would be willing to speak with other instructors about having these students enroll in classes. However, two of the instructors felt that the BCPS support staff was drawing too much attention to the students with disabilities in their classes. One instructor made a comment that he thought the student with the disability in his class didn't need to have a support person in the class with him any more. Based on these responses, the coordinator decided to observe the students taking college classes and determine if their levels of support needs had changed. In addition, the coordinator contacted the instructors to thank them for their feedback and to discuss how support persons could be more discreet and blend in with the classes. A meeting was held with all support staff to discuss how to implement the needed changes in student support in college classes. Once the changes were implemented, the coordinator again contacted the two instructors to see how things were going. The BCPS staff members know that keeping the lines of communication open and getting participant input throughout the year are vital to maintaining the partnerships that make the provision of transition services at the college possible.

Obviously, follow-up on students who have exited school can be conducted once a year for several years.

Creating a schedule ensures not only that evaluation will be conducted at a convenient time of the year but also that it is part of daily operations. It may be wise to avoid scheduling evaluation activities during months that are busy paperwork times. Also, the progress and problems identified through the evaluations should be shared with the advisory committee. Based on the feedback received, overall goals or practices may need to be revised, which will require additional meetings of the staff and committee members.

Assign Personnel to Collect and Compile Data

Different evaluation activities may be assigned to various personnel. For example, documentation of student and staff activities could be collected weekly or monthly by staff members and reviewed quarterly by the coordinator. Evaluations of student, parent, or employer satisfaction could be done biannually or annually by the coordinator. Form 34 contains space to assign a person or persons to conduct each of the evaluation activities.

The persons responsible for conducting each form of evaluation should be asked to share their findings with the advisory committee on an annual basis. Evaluation activities may also be conducted by individuals not directly involved in service provision. Community agency personnel or local university or college faculty members could be contracted to conduct an external evaluation. An external evaluation may not be needed annually, but one conducted every 3 to 5 years would provide an objective measure of the activities, outcomes, and level of satisfaction with the services provided in the college or community site.

Review and Share Evaluation Data

Once the evaluation data are collected, they should be compiled and reviewed at least once a year by staff and advisory committee members. To make the review process easier, one committee member should be asked to organize a packet. He or she may use Form 35: Checklist of Evaluation Documents (see p. 106) for this purpose. This packet will provide a comprehensive overview of all the information used to review transition services in the college or community setting.

A review of student and staff activities will allow the advisory committee to monitor student achievements and outcomes, determine if goals have been met, and identify and prioritize continuing needs. This information will also help indicate whether changes are needed in terms of adding more staff, changing staff responsibilities, changing the focus of service delivery (e.g., develop more employment sites), or identifying more inclusive college or community linkages. Once all data are reviewed, the advisory committee members can decide if the major service-delivery goals have been achieved. In addition, they will be able to assess whether the current evaluation methods are adequate or different measures should be employed in the following year. A new evaluation schedule for the following year should then be created.

The results of evaluation activities should also be shared with key school administrators and other stakeholders (e.g., parent groups, funding agencies). Both goals and objectives that were achieved and ones that were not accomplished should be documented. Providing school administrators and college personnel with both positive and negative feedback offers a realistic picture of how transition services in college or community settings are provided. Feedback also may be vital in securing additional resources and staff members needed to support students with significant disabilities in college and community settings.

APPENDIX

Chapter 3
Reproducible Forms

Form 23: Compilation of Student Activities
20__–20__ School Year

Date:

Name and Title of Person Completing Form:

Student Activities

Fill in the blank for each of the following questions:

<table>
<tr>
<td>

_____ Total number of students served

_____ Number of students who attended college/adult education courses for credit

_____ Number of students who attended college/adult education courses for audit

_____ Number of students participating in college courses informally

_____ Number of students receiving certification

_____ Number of students regularly ($\geq$ 2x/mo) participating in clubs and organizations on campus

</td>
<td>

_____ Number of students regularly participating ($\geq$ 2x/mo) in recreational activities in the community

_____ Number of students working full time

_____ Average rate of pay (FT)

_____ Number of students working part time

_____ Average rate of pay (PT)

_____ Number of students in unpaid training sites

_____ Average hours of job support from staff

_____ Number of students receiving services from agencies serving adults

</td>
</tr>
</table>

List college courses taken:

Other:

List paid job locations:

List clubs/organizations accessed on campus:

List community recreation facilities accessed:

Recommendations for changes/improvements:

Recommended changes in goals:

Note. Compile information from Forms 19–21 in Chapter 2 on this form.

Form 24: Compilation of Student Goal Achievement
20__–20__ School Year

Student Name	Date	# of Goals Met	# of Goals Unmet	Unmet Goals(s) and Reason	Response to Unmet Goals

Total number of goals met:

Total number of goals not met:

Form 25: Compilation of Staff Activities
20__–20__ School Year

Date:

Name and Title of Person Completing Form:

Staff Activities

Fill in the percentage of time spent on the following activities:

	In-Class Support	College Class Support	Employment Support	Community Access	Transportation (Travel Training)	Networking	Data Collection	Administrative Duties	Other
Coordinator									
Support Staff									
Average									

The majority of staff time is spent on:

More staff time is needed for the following activities:

Less staff time should be spent on the following activities:

Recommendation for changes in staffing or staff activities:

Note. Compile information from Form 22 in Chapter 2 on this form.

Form 26: Student Exit Information

Date Completed: _____

Completed by: _____

Student Name:		Address:			Currently Employed As:
Telephone No.:		E-Mail Address:			Other Contact:
Parents' Names:	Mother's Work Phone No.:	Father's Work Phone No.:	Date of Exit:	Age at Exit:	Current Service Agency:
Mother's E-Mail Address:		Father's E-Mail Address:		Support Received from: VR DDA SSI SSDI	Contact Person and Phone No.:
Start Date:	Rate of Pay:	Hours Worked per Week:	Benefits Received: ☐ Medical ☐ Vacation Other:		Comments:
Current Living Situation:	Current Rent:	Plans for Future Living Situation:			Comments:
Current Continuing Education:		Plans for Future Continuing Education			Comments:
Current Community Activities:		Plans for Future Community Participation:			Comments:

Note. VR = Vocational Rehabilitation; DDA = Developmental Disabilities Administration; SSI = Supplemental Securities Income; SSDI = Social Security Disability Insurance.

Form 27: Follow-Up Information

Date Completed: _____

Completed by: _____

Student Name:			Address: Check If Changed ☐	Other Contact:
Telephone No.:			E-Mail Address:	
Parents' Names:	Mother's Work Phone No.:	Father's Work Phone No.:	Date of Contact:	Method of Contact:	Person Contacted	Currently Employed As: Check If Changed ☐
If New, Reason for Leaving Previous Employment:	Start Date:	Rate of Pay:	Hours Worked per Week:	Benefits Received: ☐ Medical ☐ Vacation Other	Receives Support from: VR DDA SSI SSDI	Current Agency: Check If Changed ☐ Contact Person and Phone No.: If New, Student's Reason for Leaving Previous Agency:
Current Living Situation:			Plans for Future Living Situation:		Comments:
Current Rent:					
Current Continuing Education:			Plans for Future Continuing Education:		Comments:
Current Community Activities:			Plans for Future Community Participation:		Comments:

Note. VR = Vocational Rehabilitation; DDA = Developmental Disabilities Administration; SSI = Supplemental Securities Income; SSDI = Social Security Disability Insurance.

Form 28: Compilation of Follow-Up Information

School: _____

Month/Year Data Collected	Number of Graduates	Graduates Employed	Graduates Receiving Benefits	Avg/Rate of Pay	Avg. Hours/Wk.	Graduates Unemployed	Receiving Vocational Rehabilitation Services	Receiving Developmental Disabilities Administration Services	Receiving Supplemental Security Income Services	Living with Family	Living in Community w/Support	Living Independently	Enrolled in Continuing Education	Participating in Community Activities

Form 29: Parent Survey

Directions: We are interested in your opinion about the transition program in which your son or daughter participates. Please answer the following statements by circling the letter that indicates your level of agreement with each statement:

(A) Strongly Agree (B) Agree (C) Don't Know (D) Disagree (E) Strongly Disagree (N/A) Not Applicable

1. My son or daughter enjoys receiving services at the transition program.

    A   B   C   D   E

2. I wish that my son or daughter had stayed in his or her high school program.

    A   B   C   D   E

3. My son or daughter has demonstrated an increase in independence since attending this program.

    A   B   C   D   E

4. My son or daughter's self-esteem has improved through attending this program.

    A   B   C   D   E

5. My son or daughter has made new friends while attending the program.

    A   B   C   D   E

6. My son or daughter has demonstrated an increase in age-appropriate social skills.

    A   B   C   D   E

7. I am satisfied with the college course selections offered to my son or daughter.

    A   B   C   D   E   N/A

8. I am satisfied with the job sites offered to my son or daughter in the community or at the college.

    A   B   C   D   E   N/A

9. I am satisfied with the progress my son or daughter is making toward achieving IEP objectives.

    A   B   C   D   E

10. I am satisfied with the level of communication from the staff.

    A   B   C   D   E

The things I like most are:

The things I like least are:

Form 30: Student Survey

Directions: Please answer the following items:

I enjoy going to the transition program.   Yes ___   No ___

I enjoy going to school more this year than last year.   Yes ___   No ___

I would rather be in my home high school.   Yes ___   No ___

I am happy with the college classes I take at the transition
program.   Yes ___   No ___   N/A ___

My favorite class is: _____ .

My instructors treat me: ___ well   ___ okay   ___ poorly

I am afraid to ask for assistance from the college teachers.   Yes ___   No ___   N/A ___

I feel the class work is too hard for me.   Yes ___   No ___

I feel better about myself because of attending this program. Yes ___   No ___

I have made new friends this year.   Yes ___   No ___

I miss my friends from high school.   Yes ___   No ___

I have more friends now than I did in high school.   Yes ___   No ___

I like my job.   Yes ___   No ___

I wish I had a different job.   Yes ___   No ___

I am learning to be more independent this year.   Yes ___   No ___

I have learned how to set goals for myself.   Yes ___   No ___

I have learned to be more active in my IEP meetings.   Yes ___   No ___

What I like most:

What I like least:

Form 31: Peer Survey

Directions: We are interested in your opinion about the students with disabilities who are receiving transition services at your college. Answer the following statements by circling the letter that best indicates your level of agreement with each statement or by placing a check mark by "Yes" or "No" for statements 7–10.

(A) Strongly Agree   **(B) Agree**   **(C) Don't Know**   **(D) Disagree**   **(E) Strongly Disagree**

1. Students with disabilities are welcome at this institution.

   A   B   C   D   E

2. Students with disabilities are able to benefit from taking classes here.

   A   B   C   D   E

3. The presence of students with disabilities in my class had a negative effect on my ability to learn.

   A   B   C   D   E

4. The presence of students with disabilities in my class made me feel uncomfortable.

   A   B   C   D   E

5. The students with disabilities have a positive influence on the class.

   A   B   C   D   E

6. My understanding of the capabilities of students with disabilities has increased since I took a class with these students.

   A   B   C   D   E

7. I have become friends with a student with a disability.   Yes _____   No _____

8. I have attended a social event with a student with a disability on or off campus.   Yes _____   No _____

9. I would be interested in learning more about the services provided to students with disabilities here at the college.   Yes _____   No _____

10. I would be interested in becoming a peer tutor.   Yes _____   No _____

Comments:

Form 32: Faculty and Staff Survey

Directions: We are interested in your input regarding the presence of students from the transition program. Please fill in your answers to the statements listed below.

Instructor Name: Courses Taught:

Number of Students   Student Supports
with Disabilities Enrolled: Provided by:

1. As a result of students' participating in my class, I have made changes to my:

    _____ Tests   If so, how? _____

    _____ Assignments   If so, how? _____

    _____ Lecture Style   If so, how? _____

    _____ Pacing   If so, how? _____

2. The staff or peer helpers assigned to my class:

    _____ a. provide too much attention to the student with disabilities

    _____ b. are a distraction to my class

    _____ c. contribute to the class

    _____ d. help me in teaching

    _____ e. help other students in the class

3. I feel that I understand the needs of students
    with disabilities in my class.   Yes _____   No _____

4. I would like further information about how to
    serve students with disabilities in my class.   Yes _____   No _____

5. I would be willing to talk to other professors/
    instructors about students with disabilities
    enrolling in their classes.   Yes _____   No _____

Suggestions/Comments:

Form 33: Satisfaction Data Summary

Student Input

Strengths:

Suggested Needs:

Family Input

Strengths:

Suggested Needs:

Faculty and Staff Input

Strengths:

Suggested Needs:

Peer Input

Strengths:

Suggested Needs:

Area(s) of Greatest Satisfaction:

Area(s) of Least Satisfaction:

Recommended Changes:

Form 34: Evaluation Activities Schedule

Directions: Check off evaluation activities to be conducted and indicate the person who will conduct the activity, how often the activity will be conducted, and how data are to be collected.

Evaluation Activity	Person Responsible	Schedule (Annually, Monthly, Biweekly)	Method of Data Collection or Form Used
Monitoring			
Student Activities			
Student Goals			
Staff Activities			
Compilation			
Outcomes			
Student Exit Information			
Follow Along			
Satisfaction			
Student			
Parent			
Peers			
College Personnel			
Summary Report			
External Evaluation			
Compile Evaluation Documents			
Data Review			

Form 35: Checklist of Evaluation Documents

Name of Program:

Coordinator:

School Year: 20____–20____

Meeting Date:

Committee Members:

_____   _____

_____   _____

_____   _____

_____   _____

_____   _____

Compile a packet of the following documents to be reviewed annually by the advisory committee:

1. List of Goals

2. Form 23: Compilation of Student Activities

3. Form 24: Compilation of Student Goal Achievement

4. Form 25: Compilation of Staff Activities

5. Form 26: Student Exit Information

6. Form 27: Follow-Up Information

7. Form 28: Compilation of Follow-Up Information

8. Form 33: Satisfaction Data Summary

9. Form 34: Evaluation Activities Schedule

10. Other:

11. Other:

Bibliography

Agran, M., Snow, K., & Swaner, J. (1999). A survey of secondary level teachers' opinions on community-based instruction and inclusive education. *Journal of the Association for Persons with Severe Handicaps, 24,* 58–62.

Bishop, K. D., Amate, S. L., & Villalobos, P. J. (1995). Post-secondary considerations. In M. A. Falvey (Ed.), *Inclusive and heterogeneous schooling: Assessment, curriculum, and instruction* (pp. 363–393). Baltimore: Brookes.

Doyle, M. B. (2003). "We want to go to college too": Supporting students with significant disabilities in higher education. In D. L. Ryndak & S. Alper (Eds.), *Curriculum and instruction for students with significant disabilities in inclusive settings* (pp. 307–322). Boston: Pearson Education.

Fisher, D., & Sax, C. (1999). Noticing differences between secondary and post-secondary education: Extending Agran, Snow, and Swaner's discussion. *Journal of the Association for Persons with Severe Handicaps, 24,* 303–305.

Grigal, M., & Neubert, D. A. (2004). Parents' inschool values and postschool expectations for transition aged youth with disabilities. *Career Development for Exceptional Individuals, 27,* 65–85.

Grigal, M., Neubert, D. A., & Moon, M. S. (2001). Public school programs for students with significant disabilities in post-secondary settings. *Education and Training in Mental Retardation and Developmental Disabilities, 36,* 244–254.

Grigal, M., Neubert, D. A., & Moon, M. S. (2002). Postsecondary options for students with significant disabilities. *Teaching Exceptional Children, 35*(2), 68–73.

Hall, M., Kleinert, H. L., & Kearns, F. J. (2000). Going to college! Post-secondary programs for students with moderate and severe disabilities. *Teaching Exceptional Children, 32*(3), 58–65.

Hamill, L. B. (2003). Going to college: The experiences of a young woman with Down syndrome. *Mental Retardation, 41,* 340–353.

Hart, D., Mele-McCarthy, J., Pasternack, R. H., & Zimbrich, K. (2004). Community college: A pathway to success for youth with learning, cognitive, and intellectual disabilities in secondary settings. *Education and Training in Developmental Disabilities, 39,* 54–66.

Hart, D., Zafft, C., & Zimbrich, K. (2001). Creating access to college for all students. *Journal for Vocational Special Needs Education, 23*(2), 19–30.

Moon, M. S., Grigal, M., & Neubert, D. A. (2001). High school and beyond. *Exceptional Parent, 31*(1), 52–57.

National Center for the Study of Post-Secondary Educational Supports. (2000). *National survey of educational support provision to students with disabilities in post-secondary education settings.* Honolulu: University of Hawaii at Manoa, National Center for the Study of Post-Secondary Educational Supports.

National Clearinghouse on Post-Secondary Education for Individuals with Disabilities. (2000, December). *Pathways to employment: Nondegree post-secondary options for individuals with developmental disabilities* (Part II). Retrieved December 10, 2001, from http://www.heath.gwu.edu/info-from-heath/dec00.html

National Council on Disability and Social Security Administration. (2000). *Transition and postschool outcomes for youth with disabilities: Closing the gaps to post-secondary education and employment.* Washington, DC: Author.

National Transition Alliance. (2000, June). 1999 selected model programs/promising practices. *Alliance Newsletter, 4,* 3–15.

Neubert, D. A., Moon, M. S., & Grigal, M. (2002). Post-secondary education and transition services for students ages 18–21 with significant disabilities. *Focus on Exceptional Children, 34,* 1–11.

Neubert, D. A., Moon, M. S., & Grigal, M. (2004). Activities of students with significant disabilities in postsecondary settings. *Education and Training in Developmental Disabilities, 39,* 16–25.

Neubert, D. A., Moon, M. S., Grigal, M., & Redd, V. (2001). Post-secondary educational practices for individuals with mental retardation and other significant disabilities: A review of the literature. *Journal of Vocational Rehabilitation, 16,* 155–168.

Page, B., & Chadsey-Rusch, J. (1995). The community college experience for students with and without disabilities: A viable transition outcome? *Career Development for Exceptional Individuals, 18,* 85–95.

Patton, J. R., Smith, T. E. C., Clark, G. M., Polloway, E. A., Edgar, E., & Lee, S. (1996). Individuals with mild mental retardation: Post-secondary outcomes and implications for educational policy. *Education and Training in Mental Retardation and Developmental Disabilities, 31,* 75–85.

Smith, T. E. C., & Puccini, I. K. (1995). Position statement: Secondary curricula and policy issues for students with MR. *Education and Training in Mental Retardation and Developmental Disabilities, 30,* 275–282.

TASH. (2000). *The TASH resolution on the people for whom TASH advocates.* Retrieved April 14, 2004, from http://tash.org/resolutions/res02advocate.htm.

Tashie, C., Malloy, J. M., & Lichtenstein, S. J. (1998). Transition or graduation? Supporting all students to plan for the future. In C. J. Jorgensen (Ed.), *Restructuring high schools for all students: Taking students to the next level* (pp. 234–259). Baltimore: Brookes.

Weir, C. (2004). Person centered and collaborative supports for college success. *Education and Training in Developmental Disabilities, 39,* 67–73.

Workforce Investment Act, 29 U.S.C. § 765, 1998.

Zafft, C. (2002). *A case study of student–parent–faculty–DSO specialist unites postsecondary education project.* Unpublished manuscript, University of Hawaii, Honolulu.

Zafft, C., Hart, D., & Zimbrich, K. (2004). College career connection: A study of youth with intellectual disabilities and the impact of postsecondary education. *Education and Training in Developmental Disabilities, 39,* 45–53.

WEB SITES

On-Campus Outreach, Department of Special Education, University of Maryland. Available: http://www.education.umd.edu/oco

Transition Coalition, University of Kansas. Available: http://www.transitioncoalition.org

About the Authors

Meg Grigal, PhD, is the co–principal investigator and project director of On-Campus Outreach, an OSEP-funded outreach project at the University of Maryland. For the past 5 years, she has provided technical assistance and training for personnel in the United States on the provision of transition services to students with significant disabilities in postsecondary settings and has published numerous articles on the topic. As a research associate in the Department of Special Education at the University of Maryland for the past 8 years, she has taught coursework and coordinated multiple personnel preparation grants in transition. Dr. Grigal has conducted and published research in the areas of transition planning, self-determination, inclusion, and the use of person-centered planning techniques. She is committed to working with families, professionals, and individuals with disabilities to help them achieve their desired outcomes in life.

Debra A. Neubert, PhD, has been an associate professor in the Department of Special Education at the University of Maryland in College Park for the past 18 years. She teaches undergraduate and graduate courses in secondary special education and transition services. Dr. Neubert is the principal investigator for On-Campus Outreach, a federally funded outreach project designed to investigate practices and outcomes for students with significant disabilities ages 18 to 21 years who receive special education services at postsecondary sites. Her other interests center on transition assessment, assistive technology, program evaluation, and assistance to families in including students with disabilities in the general education curriculum.

M. Sherril Moon, EdD, has been a professor of special education at the University of Maryland for the past 15 years. Her teaching, research, and community service over the past 30 years have focused on the transition of young adults from school to adulthood, employment of adults with severe disabilities, and integration of school and community recreation for people with disabilities. She coauthored two of the first texts on supported employment and transition and has published many other works related to supporting people with disabilities at school, work, and play. Dr. Moon is currently training special educators and working as an advocate for students with disabilities and their families. She has provided training to professionals, parents, and advocates across the country.